Leave

the

Light

On

ENERGY HEALING
PSYCHIC DEVELOPMENT

Leave the Light On

An Alchemist's Guide to
Turning Trauma into a Sacred Gift

Written and Illustrated
by Kathy Lamm

To survive the darkness of her childhood,
she had to learn to see in it.
Now, she teaches others how to find the
light within their own wounds.

A Note to the Reader

The story you are about to read is a collection of my memories, recalled to the best of my ability. Memory is a subjective landscape, and others involved in these events—my siblings, my family—may remember them differently. This, however, is my truth. To honor the privacy of those involved, I have changed the names of the people within these pages.

In telling this story, I have also purposely chosen not to identify my sexual abuser. Who he was is not important to the narrative of how my psychic abilities developed. The abuse was a catalyst, but this is not his story. It is the story of how a wound can be turned into a sacred gift.

To my father:
The melody in my mind is
your creative spirit.

To my husband:
The rhythm of my life is
your beating heart.

To my sons:
The reason for my story is
your beautiful world.

Table of Contents

The First Ghost

There are stories that live in the bones of a family, told so often they become a kind of ghost, haunting the quiet spaces between what is said and what is felt. The story of my birth was one of those ghosts. My dad was its keeper, and he would conjure it for me throughout my life, never seeming to grasp the deep, traumatic harm it caused—a wound in the very architecture of our beginning.

He'd always start the same way. "When we brought you home from the hospital," he'd say, his voice a mixture of wonder and old pain, "you refused to be held."

In his telling, I was a tiny enigma. I would scream when laid in my crib, a raw, desperate sound. But when picked up, the screaming would intensify, my entire body stiffening into a rigid arch of protest. My mother, he said, was devastated. This was her firstborn, the child she had carried and dreamed of, and my tiny body was rejecting her touch. The thread of the maternal bond, supposed to be woven in those first moments of skin-on-skin contact, was already fraying. What she couldn't know was that I wasn't rejecting her; I was rejecting the agony that had become my entire world.

The reason was discovered shortly after: a deadly case of bacterial spinal meningitis, likely contracted during birth. I was rushed back to the hospital, a blur of sterile hands and panicked voices. There, under the harsh fluorescent lights, I was put on a heavy course of intravenous antibiotics. The doctors warned my parents that I might not survive and, if I did, there was a fifty-fifty chance of permanent brain damage.

"You were so tiny," my dad would continue, the memory still vivid in his eyes. "They had to put needles all over your head with wires connected to them. It looked like spaghetti." He would usually chuckle at that image, a nervous laugh to soften the horror of it. But his tone always turned serious for the next part. "It was so hard to leave you there. The doctors told us we couldn't hold you, and seeing you like that just broke our hearts. We decided it was better to leave you in their care."

So I spent the first weeks of my life in a Florida hospital, a universe of sensation reduced to a single, sharp point of pain. My world was the cold of a metal table, the prick of needles, the disembodied voices of nurses, and the constant, lonely ache of an untouched body. Strapped down with feeding tubes and IVs, I believe I was already having second thoughts about coming into this world. I was also, I think, already learning my first psychic lesson: when the physical world is unbearable, you must find a way to leave it. My spirit began its long practice of disconnecting, of floating above the pain because it could not endure it.

"When we finally brought you home for good, you had no voice," my dad recalled. "You had screamed so much in the hospital that you'd lost it completely." The silence that followed those weeks became the second ghost in our story. "We had to let you sleep in bed with us because we couldn't hear you cry. We could only tell by looking at you.

Not a single sound came out," he would exclaim, his voice softening as he shook his head in lingering disbelief. "It was the strangest thing."

A voice stolen. A bond severed. I have few memories of my mother before the age of five, but I feel the echo of that initial silence. It is the emptiness where a secure attachment should be. I would learn later about bonding impairment and attachment disorders, the clinical terms for a wound that felt primal. The lack of that secure base manifested as a host of problems later in life, but as a child, it was just a constant, unnamed ache—the feeling of being fundamentally alone.

My mom must have been struggling, too, lost in her own silent scream. I can only imagine the storm of guilt, fear, and inadequacy that raged within her. She may have suffered from a severe postpartum depression that spiraled into a crisis she could never overcome. Back then, such things were not discussed. A mother's pain was a private shame, to be hidden away.

Years later, after my dad died, I was sorting through the archaeology of his life—old photos, letters, and official papers. In a dusty box, I found a stack of brittle, yellowed telegrams he had received while deployed on the USS Saratoga.

The thin paper felt like a ghost's skin in my hands. The words painted a stark picture of reality. She was twenty-four years old, alone with five children to care for. She had no money, no husband to hold her, and no hope for support. The impossible weight of it all must have crushed her. Perhaps, in her mind, the thread of our bond had not just frayed, but snapped completely.

This, I believe, was the beginning of her own unraveling, the moment she began to disappear long before she ever walked out the door.

PART I

The Unraveling

To understand the alchemy, you must first witness the wound. I invite you to step back in time with me, into the quiet, dark rooms of my childhood where a little girl learned that monsters were real and safety was an illusion. This is the story of how a family, and a soul, began to unravel.

CHAPTER ONE

Leave the Light On

Oh, no. The hall light is off again.

Leave the light on! I scream in silence.

Just breathe. But I have to pee. Just breathe. But my stomach is growling so loud.

Shhhh… be very still. I have to be quiet, but my stomach isn't listening.

I lie there. In silence, holding my breath, trying to focus my eyes. The shadows and shadow lights slowly waltz across the items in my room softly and dimly illuminating muted details. I strain to make out the softened outlines of various pieces of furniture within the room. The tall, wide dresser beside my bed. Its overwhelming size blocks out what little light is coming from the hall creating a deep dark abyss that often serves as a hiding spot for an uninvited nighttime visitor.

My senses stretch, caught in a cycle of straining to see into the darkness, listening for the most minute sound, and feeling for any unwanted presence.

My stomach lets out a long, agonizing moan. The sound pierces the silence, filling me with a sharp, anxious fear.

Have you ever been so hungry that your entire body hurts? It's a different kind of hunger. Your stomach twists and tightens, growling out in slow, deep, breathless waves of pain. You try to will it away, but there is no silencing it. This is the kind of hunger that comes from not eating for days, a hunger that spans months and years of neglect.

I remember my granny's famous coffee biscuit breakfast. It was my favorite. I remember the bitter smell of warm fresh coffee wafting through the house, the scent of freshly made buttermilk biscuits, my granny's smile, her round face covered in flour. She had been up for hours. There's a small radio on the counter playing gospel music. She hums along with the occasional chorus breaking through in song. I clear the sleep from my eyes as she places a huge mug of coffee on the table in front of me.

"Are you hungry, hun?" she asked.

"I am, Granny," I reply eagerly.

She breaks apart the warm biscuit fresh from the oven, dropping the fluffy white pieces into the mug. As it sinks into the dark liquid, she adds heavy cream, a generous spoonful of sugar, and a sprinkle of cinnamon on top. "Here you go, darling. Enjoy," she says, patting my head and leaving a little puff of flour floating in the air.

I wish for a cup of my granny's coffee biscuit now. My mouth waters as a single tear traces a path down my cheek.

My dad taught me that if you count the seconds between a flash of lightning and the sound of thunder, you can tell how far away the storm is. I remember standing with him in the field by Granny's house, watching a distant storm as dark, rolling clouds consumed the sky.

A flash of light. "You see that?" he'd said. "Just count."

"One Mississippi, two Mississippi, three Mississippi…" I counted. Then, CRASH—a loud roar of thunder.

"See? That means the storm is three miles away," he told me. He pointed to the nearby trees. "Do you see the leaves? They've flipped upside down, showing the lighter color of their undersides. That's because the wind is blowing in the opposite direction. That's how you know a storm is coming." He'd smiled with a slight giggle as I watched the leaves dance and hum a loud, shushing sound in the wind.

What would he say it means to count the space between stomach growls? Mine hurts so badly, and I still can't stop thinking about how much I have to pee.

One Mississippi, two Mississippi, three Mississippi…

I wish my dad were here. He's been out to sea for months; I can't even remember what he looks like. He's in the Navy, stationed on a ship somewhere far away. I know if he were here, I wouldn't be hungry. He knew what real hardship was. His story was carved into a mountainside in the Appalachians, a rugged passage known as Buffalo Gap. He was one of thirteen children raised under a single, tin roof, where the running brook was their only water source and hunger was a constant negotiation.

He inherited his parents' grit, but in him, it blossomed into a restless fire. He hunted rattlesnakes for a living, his first lesson in coaxing miracles from death. That fire eventually led him to the Navy, away from the mountains, and into the arms of a woman he rushed to marry, so desperate was he to build the family he never truly had. He even fought to keep her children when they weren't his own. He would never let us starve. I wonder if he knows we don't have any food, or that we don't know where Mom is. I wonder if he knows why I'm afraid all the time.

How do other adults not know? Do they not see me? Is it that easy to look away from the little wallflower girl in tattered, dirty hand-me-downs two sizes too big? Is it easy to dismiss my swollen stomach and the dark circles under my sunken eyes? The girl who never smiles, who never laughs. Can they not see I'm starving? Can they not see I'm suffering? Can they not see I'm all alone?

Maybe it's just easier for them to pretend I'm not here.

I pray in the darkness. I pray for school to start soon. I hate summer. At least at school, I get to eat lunch. My favorite cafeteria food is applesauce. It reminds me of Granny and the apple orchard beside her house where I used to run and play with my cousins. I'd climb a tree, pick an apple, and eat it right then and there, the sticky juice running down my chin and creating a magnet for dirt.

I could never understand why my mom would leave for days at a time and return without food. Where did she go? Did she eat? When she was home, she was either drunk, crying, sleeping, or fighting with my older brother and sister. I'm not sure she even knew I was there. I was six years old, and no one knew I existed.

Wait. I hear something.

My eyes see nothing but deeper shadows in the already pitch-black room. Is that… footsteps? My breath hitches. I know what's coming. Why can't I just disappear? No one sees me anyway.

If I concentrate, I can become aware of the other rooms in the house. I can see who is in them and what they are doing. I can feel their feelings and know their thoughts. It's how I keep myself safe—by knowing. I reach out with my mind, feeling for their presence, trying to discern the intent behind those soft, approaching sounds.

The floorboards creak, closer now. My heart pounds against my ribs, a frantic drum in the silent house. I'm not alone. I feel a bad, slow feeling— his air feels sticky and mean. Cold, sharp fear pierces through hunger.

I squeeze my eyes shut. Tighter. Maybe if I try really hard, I can disappear. Just melt into the mattress, become one with the shadows until he leaves. The footsteps stop just outside my door. I hold my breath, willing my growling stomach to be silent, willing myself invisible. I know if he comes in, there will be no escape. I pray for my dad, for school, for anyone to see me, to save me from the darkness that always finds me, even when the light is supposed to be on.

I disappear.

I feel myself disconnecting from my body, whisked away in the vision of a starling in flight. Like quicksilver in a sunbeam, I dart and turn, a miniature ballerina swirling weightlessly through the crystal blue sky. Each flick of my wing is a whisper as I paint the air with thousands of other tiny dancers. Then, a sudden, sweeping shift—a collective breath as a thousand hearts merge into one, a divine choreography that transmutes space and time.

Is this the way to heaven?

I begin to hear the music of angels as I travel deeper into the spirit of all creation. Heaven must be a real place, far beyond this human experience, far beyond pain, hunger, and silent suffering. A place of perfect peace and joy, where life is free from the limitations of this world.

If only I could stay there.

I wake to Marian screaming, "Kathy peed the bed again!"

CHAPTER TWO

The Secret

The school year is almost over. I enjoy school; learning keeps my mind active, and a seven-year-old shouldn't have this much to think about.

Today, I'm just tired.

I sit with my elbows on the desk, fists pressed so tightly against my temples that my knuckles turn white and my fingertips go numb. My gaze is unfocused, staring at the paper Mrs. Martin passed out at the beginning of class. We're supposed to be studying the words on the page, memorizing them for our weekly spelling test, but I can't make them out. The letters blur together into squiggly lines. My head feels heavy. I sense myself slipping away as my blinks slow and my eyelids become impossible to keep open.

"Miss Edmund." The words sound like they're coming from a distant dream. "Miss Edmund, did you do your homework?"

Mrs. Martin's voice sharpens into focus. I reach into my desk and pull out the assignment. The paper is crinkled, with small tears along the edge where I ripped it from a spiral notebook. I had written my ten spelling words ten times each, but my handwriting was messy, the soft pencil smeared across the page. I still don't understand how writing words over and over helps you learn to spell.

I walk to the front of the class and place my paper in the tray on her desk.

"Did you get enough sleep last night?" she asks in her soft, compassionate voice.

I nod without lifting my head to meet her eyes. It feels like my head is a giant orange balanced on a toothpick, swirling dramatically in compliance.

"Try to get to bed earlier tonight, okay, Miss Edmund?"

Again, I manage a slight, less enthusiastic nod. She's right, I didn't get much sleep. I was out of my body for much longer than usual last night. But that's not something I can tell Mrs. Martin. I slowly walk back to my desk.

I can't remember the last time I saw my mom. I try to think hard about it. Was it last week? The other day? I just don't know. Maybe she's upstairs sleeping. Sometimes I find her asleep on the sofa, and if I try to wake her, she only responds with a grunt or groan.

When I get home from school, my sister Lydia is waiting. She asks how my day was.

"I was tired," I told her.

"Well, get your homework done so you can get a bath and go to bed early," she says.

I don't bother asking if there's anything to eat. I can see in her eyes that there isn't. Although Lydia is only six years older than me, she looks like an adult. Her face is worn, and dark circles surround the profound sorrow in her eyes. Her thin, blonde hair is a messy chop, with uneven strands falling across her forehead where she obviously cut it herself. She is always kind and gentle with me, but I feel her pain like a blade slowly carving through my heart. There's nothing I can say. I can't tell her why I'm so tired; she's tired, too. I can't tell her I'm hungry; she's just as hungry. I can't tell her I feel so alone when I can feel the loneliness radiating from her soul.

She sits on the closed toilet lid, watching me as I bathe. "I know you're hungry, but you can't tell anyone, okay?" she says quietly. "And don't tell anyone that Mom isn't here. Just tell them she's sleeping or had to run to the store."

The thought of my mom going to the store is almost funny; I don't remember her ever going to a store. But I sense the fear in Lydia's voice and understand, somehow, how much trouble we're in.

"If you tell anyone," she continues, her voice barely a whisper, "they will take you away. They'll separate all of us, and we won't ever see each other again."

I don't want that. Where would they take us? To jail? Would they put Lydia in jail? What about my brothers? My youngest brother, River, is only two. Would they put a two-year-old in jail? And my little sister? She drives me crazy, but I don't want her to go to jail.

I finish my bath and go to bed. I pray. I pray for sleep, for something to eat, and for none of us to go to jail.

CHAPTER THREE

A Summer Alone

I woke up late and rushed to get dressed for school. My first thought was to help Marian, my younger sister. I picked out a shirt and shorts for each of us from the pile of dirty clothes in the corner of our room. Marian couldn't find her shoes. After a frantic search, I found a pair of gummy, slip-on sandals in the backyard. They were tight on her feet, and one was torn on the side, forcing her pinky toe to stick out.

She started to cry. "They don't fit me!" she exclaimed.

"We're going to miss the bus," I snapped, with no patience for her whining. "Just wear them." It was the last day of school, my last day of second grade.

Lydia must have already left; I didn't see her anywhere. That meant Mom must be home. Lydia wouldn't leave River alone in the house if no one else were here. I didn't see him either, but I assumed he was still asleep in bed with Mom. He always slept with her when she was home.

After the school year ended, my mom was home, and she seemed different. She fixed us bologna sandwiches for lunch and soup for dinner. It felt good to eat before going to bed. She wasn't drinking, but she smoked a lot. I let myself think that maybe things would be okay. I saw more of my two older brothers, Jamie and Wayne, who were rarely around when she was gone. Lydia, however, didn't trust it. She didn't talk much, just stayed in the background, watching and waiting for things to go back to the way they were.

River and Marian were happy, playing with toys as we listened to records on the record player. As each one finished, my mom replaced it with another or, more often, played the same one over and over.

We didn't have a TV—not one that worked, anyway. It had stopped working shortly after my dad was deployed, playing only loud static until my mom unplugged it for good. It still sat on the stand in the center of the living room, a constant reminder of how distant a normal childhood felt. Dad had been gone forever, it seemed. He would have liked to see us like this, acting like a real family.

I had been sleeping better, too, without a nighttime visitor. Maybe that part was over, and I could finally sleep through the night, every night.

A couple of weeks into summer break, my mom started having friends over. They stayed up late, laughing, drinking, and talking loudly. One of the men had a deep voice that echoed through the house. He sometimes spent the night sleeping on the pull-out sofa with my mom. I wanted my mom home, but I didn't want these strangers here. It made Lydia furious. She yelled at my mom, and they fought a lot.

It wasn't long before she left again. We were once again alone.

It was fun at first. We laughed and danced to the records on the turntable, playing cards and games. There was even food in the house for a little while, enough to last several days. But when the food ran out and she hadn't returned, the sadness and fear began to settle back in. It was like a familiar fog drifting down upon us, so thick it was difficult to breathe. You could taste the stagnant smoke still lingering in the air, a ghost of her brief presence.

My three older siblings found the cigarettes her friends had left behind. They smoked them at the kitchen table, talking like adults, making plans for how we were going to live on our own, how we couldn't get caught, and how we were going to get food. Wayne laid out a plan to take our lawnmower to the neighbors' houses, coughing and choking on smoke as he talked. Jamie sat quietly, not adding much, his chin raised and a cigarette held loosely between his fingers, the ash growing longer and longer at the tip. I watched anxiously, wondering when it would break and fall. Lydia bit her nails between puffs, pinching her cigarette tightly as she raised it to her puckered lips. I thought she looked like she was kissing a fish. She practiced blowing smoke rings as she and Wayne talked about the food he could buy.

They found a Ouija board one of my mom's friends must have left behind. Wayne and Lydia placed their fingertips on the plastic triangle with a bubble in it as it moved around the board. They asked silly questions, acting surprised as their own hands spelled out the answers. They played and smoked for a while, and then Wayne asked, "Will I die soon?"

The piece moved slowly across the board as the anticipation built, finally spelling its answer: Y-E-S.

Wayne jumped up, threw the board across the room, and ran out of the house into the darkness. I wasn't sure if he was ever coming back or if he was going to get killed. He seemed to really believe it.

I started to cry, an uncontrollable, sobbing cry. It wasn't just because my brother left or because the game said he was going to die. It was an angry cry. I was angry with myself. How could I let myself think everything was going to be okay? How could I believe my mom was going to be a real mother? How could I believe I wasn't going to be awakened in the darkness again?

Wayne did return, his fear eventually giving way to the more pressing matter of our hunger. The next day, he brought us bread, bologna, and a candy bar from the gas station. He had earned a few dollars mowing lawns and we were able to eat for a few more days.

The summer passed slowly. We couldn't go outside. Lydia said we had to be careful that the neighbors didn't learn we were home alone. It wasn't so bad, though. I spent most of my time drawing. I had a Barbie doll I won in a contest at school last year for guessing how many M&Ms were in a jar. I had never owned a Barbie, but I'd heard other girls talking about their Barbie houses, clothes, and boyfriends. Even though I had no one to play Barbies with, I still wanted one.

I never really made friends. I couldn't have anyone over; they would ask why my mother was never home or why we didn't have food. "They will tell their parents," Lydia would say. "And then they will come and take us away." It was okay, though. I was fine drawing and playing with my Barbie. I made her clothes from toilet paper and shoes from foil I found under the kitchen sink. My Barbie was beautiful, and I felt proud of her original wardrobe. Sometimes I drew patterns on paper towels to give her different outfits. I became crafty enough to make dresses, jumpers, pants, and jackets. She was fully outfitted and would have made the other girls with their store-bought clothes jealous.

Her mansion was a couple of shoe boxes with rooms drawn on the inside panels. I tore up old shirts to make carpets, curtains, and luxury bedding. It was a beautiful palace. My Barbie didn't need a car; she walked everywhere and enjoyed nature. Sometimes I gathered leaves from the backyard to create summer outfits for her or used sticks to build a tropical island vacation spot, complete with a pool made from a saucer filled with water. My Barbie had dark hair, just like me. She was crafty, witty, and had ingenious ideas.

CHAPTER FOUR

It's All Going to Turn Out All Right

And then it happened.

It was Sunday morning. I woke up early, filled with an urgent need to go to church. I had prayed and prayed for God to help me—prayed to not be hungry, to not be afraid, to be able to sleep without violation. But no matter how much I prayed, nothing changed.

Every Sunday, I watched Billy Graham on the tiny black and white TV I had found in my parents' room. We weren't supposed to know it was there; I discovered it one day snooping through my dad's closet. I plugged it in, and it worked. It was small and fussy, but if I moved the antenna just right, I could get enough clarity to watch Sunday Morning Passage: The Rev. Billy Graham on CBS.

I loved Rev. Billy Graham. I loved God, and watching the reverend made me feel closer to Him. He always said, "I've read the last page of the Bible. It's all going to turn out all right." I believed him. But I needed it to be okay now. I could hear his words speaking directly to me: "God has promised to supply all of our needs." "To suffer for the faith is not a penalty; it is a privilege." The power in his voice usually filled me with peace, but not this Sunday. This Sunday, I needed to go to church.

I convinced Lydia to go. We got dressed and walked out of the house to catch the church bus, the first time I had been out the front door since Mom left. Our neighbor, Mrs. Beamon, was standing in her driveway.

"Hey girls, are you heading to church?" she asked. I didn't remember her ever talking to us before.

Lydia replied with a short, sharp "yes" and a forced smile.

"That's nice," she continued, and I wished she would just stop talking. "I haven't seen your momma in a while. Is she doing okay?"

"She's sleeping," Lydia said, her voice clipped.

Mrs. Beamon started to speak again, "Well, tell her I was asking—" but Lydia cut her off.

"We're running late." She grabbed my hand, jerking my arm nearly out of its socket. "Come on."

We got on the bus and headed to church, but I didn't receive the miracle I had hoped for. In fact, I felt more anxious than ever. Lydia bit her nails and tapped her foot through the entire service. I could feel her anxiety, and so could everyone else in our pew, judging by their glaring looks and loud sighs. My own thoughts were racing so fast I barely heard a word the pastor said.

We rode the bus home in silence. Others sang joyfully, "I've got joy, joy, joy, down in my heart," but their voices didn't bring any joy to mine. I no longer felt that little light of my own. I just felt lost and wanted to disappear. I couldn't get off the bus fast enough.

As we turned the corner onto our street, I saw it: a police car parked in front of our house. My sister grabbed my hand, crushing my fingers as she picked up her pace, dragging me with her.

When we walked inside, the house was full of strangers. Mrs. Beamon was there, along with two police officers and two women I had never seen before. My brother River was sitting on the kitchen counter, and one of the women was talking to him. Marian was curled up in the corner of the stairs, and the other woman was trying to coax her down. "It's okay, honey. We're here to help," she said, but Marian just dug her face deeper into the corner.

An officer stopped Lydia at the door. "Do you know where your mom is? Are you kids here alone?" Lydia's face was white with fear. I could feel my body trembling as the other officer picked me up and set me on the counter beside River.

"Wow, you're really light for a big girl," he said. "How old are you?"

"I'm seven," I replied.

"And how old is this big guy?" he asked, pointing to River, who sat up tall with a proud smile.

"He's three," I could barely whisper.

"And is that your sister on the stairs?" I nodded. "How old is she?"

"She is five."

I heard the first officer ask Lydia, "How old are you?"

"Thirteen," she said.

"Is there anyone else here? Any other brothers or sisters?"

I heard Lydia catch her breath, unable to speak. Mrs. Beamon chimed in, "There are two older boys, but they're not here. They must have run away when they saw you pull up."

Lydia started crying, and then I started crying too.

The officer who picked me up stepped outside. The strange woman beside me patted my knee. "It's okay, honey. It's all going to turn out all right."

I instantly flashed back to Rev. Billy Graham speaking those exact words just hours earlier. Was this my fault? Did this happen because I asked God for help? I prayed for Him to help me, and now these strangers were in my kitchen saying the same things. I cried harder.

"It's okay, it's okay," she said, trying to comfort me. "Are you hungry?"

I was so hungry I couldn't speak. I just nodded.

"I'll go make them some sandwiches," Mrs. Beamon said.

I stopped sobbing long enough to choke out the question, "Are we going to jail?"

The woman chuckled softly. "Oh no, of course not, sweetheart. You didn't do anything wrong. We're here to keep you safe. We'll take care of you. It's all going to turn out all right."

Hearing Rev. Graham's words again, this time from her, began to give me some comfort. A moment later, Mrs. Beamon returned with peanut butter and jelly sandwiches, and I was so happy to see them.

CHAPTER FIVE

The In-Between

We didn't ride in the police car. Instead, we rode in a sedan with the two strange ladies from our kitchen. I knew they had told us their names, but my heart was pounding so hard I couldn't hear anything else. I wondered if a heart could explode from beating so loud. I wasn't afraid of dying. There had been many times I'd prayed for it.

On those nights, I would pray for God to let me die and return to heaven—the place Reverend Billy Graham described as being without fear, a place of love and belonging. I had never felt like I belonged anywhere. When I closed my eyes and forced myself to disappear, I imagined that place. I imagined being dead, being somewhere with no sin, no pain, no hunger, and no fear.

Because I imagined it so often, it was easy to escape there. I chose to escape now, allowing the noise of the car ride to fade away. It felt real. I found myself in a field of flowers that emitted a sweet fragrance, a cool breeze tickling the hairs on my arms while hugging me. Laughter rumbled in my belly as I remembered a joy I had long forgotten. Brightly colored trees swayed, their leaves dancing to the sound of distant birdsong. Tender white clouds drifted through an endless pale blue sky, and the warmth of the sun caressed my face. I felt my toes gliding across small river rocks covered in bright green moss as a trickling brook flowed over my feet, sending a refreshing tingle up my spine. This was heaven.

The car stopped. We were at the police station. The strange lady had promised we weren't going to jail, but here we were. I really hadn't expected anything less. Most adults lie to children.

We walked inside, and one of the ladies pointed to a row of plastic chairs against the wall. "You girls sit here."

I sat beside Lydia. She held River on her lap, still crying—not the loud sobs from before, but a shallow, sniffled cry that kept her cheeks wet and her lip trembling. I couldn't see around her, but I knew Marian was on her other side because I could hear her sucking her thumb. River sat quietly, staring at the policemen gathered around a tall desk in front of us.

The chairs were hard plastic on a wire metal frame. The chair was so cold on the back of my legs; I wished I wasn't wearing a skirt. Every time my knee touched the metal, a piercing shock screamed through my body. I trembled, unable to tell if it was from fear or the cold. We sat there forever, and I kept anticipating Barney Miller to walk out and throw us behind bars. I wondered where Jamie and Wayne were.

The next few days were a blur. We didn't go to jail, but we were all separated, just as Lydia had warned. I vaguely remember a doctor pushing on my swollen stomach and looking in my eyes, mouth, and ears. She measured my wrists, my ankles, my height, and my weight. I overheard her telling a nurse I was malnourished and needed vitamins, though I don't remember the exact words. I felt like I was only half there, trying so hard to disappear.

"Hello, Kathy. My name is Sally Hess," said a lady, greeting me as I left the exam room. She was holding Marian's hand. "Would you like to come home with me?"

No! I screamed inside. Where is Lydia? my heart cried out silently. Without a sound, I gave an uneasy nod.

"Great," she said. "Marian is excited to come too." Marian, sucking her thumb, looked at me with wide eyes that screamed we're being kidnapped. She looked far from excited. A thousand questions swirled in my head, but I didn't ask any of them: Where were we going? Who was this person? Where were River, Wayne, and Jamie? Was Wayne dead? Did my dad know what was happening?

It felt like a bad dream. The worst thing that could have happened, had happened. My older siblings had discussed this at the kitchen table. Why didn't they plan what we were supposed to do?

I disappeared.

I don't remember much about Sally Hess or her husband, John. They seemed kind, but I refused to open up. I only spoke when asked a direct question, and my answers were short and quick. I took care of Marian but barely spoke to her, either. I don't know how long we stayed with them; I tried not to think about the time passing without my consent.

One morning, Sally came into our room. "Okay, girls, let's get dressed and gather your things. You're going to stay with family now."

She didn't say who. Sally and John had bought us some new clothes and a few toys. I'd never had new clothes before. I got dressed in a new pair of shorts and a matching tank top. The top was white with little cherries on it, made of a stretchy material that formed a ruffle at the top and bottom. It had thin strings that tied into big bows on my shoulders. I had new sandals, too—ones that fit. I helped Marian get dressed, brushed our hair, and packed our few belongings into a brown paper grocery bag.

We were sitting in the lobby of a Red Cross office with Sally and John when I saw Lydia and River walk in. I was so happy I ran up and hugged them both. A few moments later, Jamie followed. I was surprised to see him. I still didn't know where Wayne was. We all sat together, waiting, and just having Lydia there gave me a sense of ease I hadn't felt since that Sunday morning.

Then, I saw them. My Granny and my Granddaddy. It felt like I hadn't seen them in years. They lived far away in the mountains; how did they even get here? I was happy to see them, but I was happier to see Lydia and River. We all stood up to greet them.

PART II

The Search for Home

Once a home is shattered, a child will spend a lifetime searching for a new one. In these next chapters, you will journey with me through that search—from the sacred sanctuary of a mountain farm to the chaos of a purple house, and into the shadow of a new mother who brought a different kind of pain. This is the search for a safe place to land.

CHAPTER SIX

The Blue Ridge

It was early, and I was in that liminal space between sleep and wakefulness. With my eyes still closed, I knew I was in my granny's house. I smelled the musky quilt, heavy on my chest, which I shared with Marian, who was still asleep in the small twin bed beside me.

I opened my eyes halfway. In the dim, golden light filtering through the small loft window, I saw Lydia asleep on the floor, wrapped in a heavy comforter. She was curled up in a ball in the corner, and the angle of the light made her look like a small sleeping bear.

The wooden floorboards beneath her varied in color, height, and width, reminding me that my granddaddy had built this house. It was a small brick farmhouse set atop a hill in the Appalachian Mountains of Western Virginia. My Pap Paw, Granny's dad, was a brick mason. "Your granddaddy and Pap Paw laid every brick in this house," Granny would say, her voice strong and proud.

The days were beginning to stretch as the sun rose across the rolling foothills of the Blue Ridge. The comfort of being in Granny's house settled deep within me; summer was fully upon us. I gazed out the tiny, open window. A cool breeze aided in the dance of the oversized sheer curtains that draped across the floor. Light glistened off the dew-covered fields, sprinkled with a few cattle beginning their morning "song." A tiny stream, rolling over stray granite boulders peeking from the earth, acted as a subtle fence, separating the fields of grazing from those of planting.

I could smell the freshly plowed fields as steam rose from the soil, and a tractor made its way over a distant hill. The sounds of chickens, pigs, and a sprightly rooster seemed far too loud for this early hour.

I heard Granny downstairs in the kitchen making breakfast—fresh biscuits to dip in cinnamon sugar and coffee with cream. The clinking of tin pots and the laughter from her and Aunt Angie were reminiscent of this carefree world. The smell of baking bread and fresh coffee wafted out the open kitchen windows, filling the air with their tantalizing scent.

My cousin Sandy and I were the first ones downstairs. "You kids take this basket and go fetch us some strawberries and blackberries for breakfast," Aunt Angie said with her deep southern drawl, handing Sandy a woven basket. "They grow down there on the side of the road," she added, pointing toward the gravel road that ran in front of the house. The road was softly carved atop the hill where my grandfather built this house and stretched on for miles.

My feet, still covered in a film of dirt from the night before, darkened as I stepped into the moist grass. We walked barefoot down to the gravel road and began walking in the ditch alongside it.

"Be careful of the poison ivy," Sandy warned. Her strawberry-blonde hair sparkled with shards of copper in the early morning sun.

Tiny freckles were sprinkled across her nose and cheeks, creating the illusion of a consistently dirty face. I watched her every step. "It's running all through these strawberries, and especially over there where the blackberries are." She pointed to a higher place in the ditch where thorny blackberry stalks grew at least ten feet tall.

We picked lots of fresh strawberries and blackberries, filling the basket. Of course, we ate a few of each, leaving red and blue sticky stains around our mouths and on our fingertips. I wiped my hands on my shirt and shorts, leaving stripes of blue and red.

Watching Sandy's fair-skinned face, I thought about how different we looked. She, like most of my Granny's family, had light hair, freckles, and blue eyes. They seemed to be made of mountain mist and sunlight. I looked down at my own skin, closer to the color of the earth, and it made me think of my dad. He was the one with Cherokee blood. "That's where you get your high cheekbones, dark eyes, and dark hair," he'd often tell me. "Our people have been here since the beginning of time. These mountains have always been our home." He'd say, "We are made of dirt, you and me," and while I never quite understood how, I knew that standing here, I felt like a part of it all.

I was happy to be here with my grandparents. Standing barefoot in the wet grass, looking out at the hazy blue mountains that stood tall, surrounding and protecting me, this world was a beautiful escape from the one I left behind. Time stood still here, and I could hear myself breathing. I felt my heart beat gently in my chest, and I knew I existed.

My Granny said that my dad was still on a ship far away and that it would be a while before he could come get us and take us home. I was happy there and didn't want to return home.

No one knew where my mother was, not even my Granny, who was her mother. She was just gone.

But it wasn't like I missed either of them. My two brothers and two sisters were there with me, along with my five cousins. Plus, I had plenty to do on the farm. My brothers, sisters, and cousins were also great playmates. The fear and anxiety I had back home had somewhat subsided.

I spent most of my days running and playing in the fields. We each had daily chores, and they changed every day. We would all take turns feeding the animals and keeping their areas clean. My least favorite chore was collecting eggs from the chicken coop. I was afraid of the chickens. They had really big, sharp talons, and they didn't like me taking their eggs. They would squawk really loud, flap their wings, and try to jump on my head. "I'm afraid they'll get caught in my hair," I'd cry.

"Get out there and get them eggs," my granny would say.

At the end of the summer, my granddaddy and uncle typically killed a few chickens for us to eat over the winter. My granddad would tuck the chicken's head under its wing and swing it around in circles until it passed out. He would then stretch its neck out on a tree stump and cut its head off with an ax. The body of the headless chicken would run around flapping its wings for what seemed like forever. It always felt as though they were chasing me. Everyone laughed at us kids being chased around the yard by bloody, headless chickens. I never liked those chickens.

Once they were dead, I'd help my granny pluck the feathers and prepare them to be put in the icebox located in the cellar under the house. Along with the icebox, we had shelves of canned vegetables from our garden. We canned tomatoes, corn, okra, beans, pickles, and even occasionally pickled pigs' feet. Well, we may have bought the pigs' feet because I don't ever remember my granddaddy killing one of our pigs, and I don't remember any missing. We also stored other salty meats there, like ham and bacon we got from the butcher.

The cellar was a scary place. It smelled bad. A light connected to an extension cord hung from the ceiling, but it was still dark, wet, it had a lot of spiders, and the occasional snake. I was always afraid of getting locked in there and no one being able to hear me scream.

The house sat atop the hill, with a huge vegetable garden at the bottom of the hill behind the house. Beside the house, beyond the pigpen, was an apple orchard that went up the side of another hill. There was a small orchard with maybe a half dozen or so apple trees. I loved apples. They smelled so good, and my granny made the best pies with them.

The sun was beginning to dip below the mountain ridge when I heard Granny holler from the back porch steps, "Edna, go down to the cellar and get a can of those tomatoes and a pack of pork chops out'd the freezer."

Granny was the only person who called me Edna. It was my first name, like hers. I didn't really like that name. It felt like a needle prick to my soul when anyone else said it. But I liked hearing it from my Granny. I could feel the love in her voice as she called out to her namesake. There was a side-mouthed smirk that came with its pronunciation.

"And get some of those snap beans out'd the field before you come up," she added as I headed down the hill to the cellar, now faced with a dilemma. Did I go to the cellar first or the field? The field was at the bottom of the hill. It was a bit challenging to climb back up the hill with my hands full, and if I had pork chops, a can of tomatoes, and enough beans for supper, I wouldn't be able to use my hands to climb. But if I went to the field first, it would be nearly dark by the time I made it up to the top of the hill where the cellar was. The light didn't always work in the cellar, and I was afraid of what else might be in the dark. I decided to go to the cellar first.

When I got down to the field, I had to lay the pork chops and the can of tomatoes in the dirt. I hadn't really considered that when I chose to go to the cellar first. I picked enough snap beans to fill my shirt, which I had pulled up to make a basket. I picked up the can of tomatoes and the pork chops. Holding them and my shirt-basket made it impossible to use my hands to climb back up the steep hill.

My bare foot slipped in loose dirt and rocks, and my knee scraped across a big, sharp rock. It began to bleed, and I wanted to cry but held it in.

By the time I got to the kitchen, blood was running down my leg, and the can of tomatoes and pack of pork chops were now covered in dirt. Granny took one look at me and started laughing. "Oh, honey, look at you," she chuckled. "You look like you fought off a bear to save our dinner. Come here and let me clean you up," she sighed.

At night, the sounds changed drastically from the day. The mating calls of frogs, crickets, and other night charmers filled the air. The nightly fire crackled as my granddaddy and uncle played their guitars and sang traditional bluegrass tunes. I assumed that alcohol enhanced the amount of laughter from the adults during those long summer nights.

Before their campfire sing-along, the adults set us up with firefly-catching gear. This consisted of a mason jar with holes punched in the lid. I always added a little grass at the bottom in case they got hungry. We were then set free in the dark mountain night to capture fireflies and fill our jars with their flickering, illuminating energy.

The night was never as dark as you would imagine. Millions of bright stars filled the sky, surrounding the biggest, brightest moon you'd ever see. It truly felt brighter than when the streetlights turned the night to day in our yard back home. Nighttime here never scared me.

Fireflies filled the air. If there was one, there were a thousand. Flashing their bright lights, flirting with invisibility, you could follow their strobe as they slowly moved through the cool night air. It was a magical dance.

The hill was filled with laughter, music, and the sounds of home. Never had I felt as "at home" as I did at this time. It was almost the end of summer. I could feel the days beginning to shorten. I started to wonder when my dad was going to come get us. There was something about time at Granny's house. It was elusive. It seemed to last forever— no real beginning or ending, just every day, different versions of the same. But when it was time to leave, it seemed like we hadn't been there long at all.

And then, he was there. I wasn't sure what to feel.

CHAPTER SEVEN

Aunt Bee's Purple House

Aunt Beatrice—Aunt Bee, as we called her—lived in a big purple house in town. The two-story wooden house had eight large-paned windows on the front, four on each side of a dark red door, stacked two over two. The white paint on the window boards was chipped and faded. Smeared paint around the edges of the panes made the frames look squiggly and lopsided. One side of the house was lower than the other, making it look as if it was sinking into the ground. The center of the roof sagged, and missing shingles left black holes.

My dad tried to open the front door, but it was stuck. The doorknob spun in his hand as he jiggled it, then thrust his shoulder into the door's center. He stumbled inside, laughing as Aunt Bee and my cousin Sammie greeted him. "Well, come on in," Aunt Bee said, lifting her arm to direct all of us inside. My four siblings and I filed into the living room, heel to toe. The house was dark and smelled like a wet forest floor.

Although the house was big, the rooms were so packed with furniture and other things that it was difficult to move through. Oversized, mismatched, dark wooden cabinets lined the walls, blocking the light from the windows. Several couches and chairs were crammed together around small tables loaded with books, magazines, and full ashtrays. Baskets of dirty plastic flowers and dust-covered knick-knacks filled the shelves and tops of the cabinets. Clothes were piled on the couches as if someone was finishing laundry, but it was obvious they had been there for some time. A musky scent of half-dried, half-dirty clothes filled the air as we passed by the piles.

The floorboards were warped, with splotches of scattered linoleum still connected in various places to the wooden planks beneath. In some spots, you could see several layers of linoleum in different patterns stacked upon each other. The edges of the torn linoleum were curled up and brittle, with missing chips that left sharp points to cut your feet when you ran barefoot through the house.

Aunt Bee had six children—all girls except for one boy. Her husband, my uncle Chase, had died when I was little. No one really talked about him, and I had never seen Aunt Bee with another man.

"Got supper on the stove. Hope y'all are hungry," Aunt Bee announced as she walked toward the kitchen at the back of the house. We all followed her through the maze-like rooms, like marching ants in search of a drop of jam. As we entered the kitchen, more cousins appeared. I suppose the mention of food had roused all the villagers. "Grab you a bowl over there," Aunt Bee waved her hand toward a stack of dishes on the counter. A precarious pile of glass and plastic plates, bowls, and cups filled the counter that looked ready to fall at the slightest tremor. Plastic forks and spoons that had obviously been used before lay at the base of the pile.

I grabbed a purple plastic bowl that had tiny white daisies melted in the plastic and the cleanest-looking spoon I could find. Each of us, bowl in hand, stepped up to Aunt Bee, who was standing over a giant pot, ladle in hand. She poured what resembled some kind of soup into my bowl. I saw corn, tomatoes, okra, pasta, peas, and carrots in a thick red sauce. "Here, get you a chicken leg," Aunt Bee said as she plopped the giant leg in my bowl, splashing tomato juice all over my face.

"What is this?" I asked, trying not to show my disgust while wiping my face.

"It's succotash," Aunt Bee said matter-of-factly. "Ain't y'all ever had succotash?" she asked. "Just try it. You'll love it. Your cousins lick the pot clean every time I make it," she said, handing me a slice of Wonder Bread.

She was right. After I got over the look of it, I loved it!

I was happy to be there with my cousins, but it was a lot different from my granny's house. We ran up and down the stairs, in and out of the house, jumped on beds, and played hide-and-seek. There was nothing stopping us from laughing and playing for hours.

That night, Aunt Bee, my dad, my other aunt, Beatty, and her husband, Chuck, were playing cards. They sat at a small card table in the corner of the dining room. Although the room was huge, so much furniture was crammed in it that there was no space to move. They laughed and smoked and talked loudly over each other. Every once in a while, Aunt Bee would scream up the steps, "You kids be quiet and stop jumpin' 'round 'fore somethin' gets broke," a statement that was immediately followed by a crashing sound. "Did y'all hear me? KEEP IT DOWN! You're not gonna want me to come up there," she bellowed, her threats repeated and empty.

"Wanna go in the backyard and look for shootin' stars?" my cousin Amber asked. By this point, I was so sweaty from jumping on the bed that I wanted to go out and cool down. We dashed past the dining room where the grown-ups were playing cards. "We're goin' outside, Maw," Amber said. They didn't even look up.

The yard was pitch black. Tall blackberry bushes towered over the tattered fence held together with twisted honeysuckle vines. We lay on the cool, tall grass, looking up at the sky. The sky in the mountains had so many more stars than the sky back home. "Look!" Amber shouted, pointing to a disappearing star that darted across the sky.

"See there?" I said. "There's another!" We lay there for the longest time, watching the stars streak across the sky.

I felt so small.

Lying there, looking up through the blackness, I tried not to think of Mom, of Wayne, of returning home. My throat got tight, and I sat up, catching my breath. "You alright?" Amber asked, patting me on the back.

"Yeah," I struggled to force out.

"You'll be alright," she said. Amber was older than me but not as old as Lydia. She had red hair with tight curls, tiny freckles on her nose and cheeks, and big hazel eyes. She reminded me of the doll my dad brought me back from Scotland. Amber didn't really fit in with the rest of us. We all had dark hair and dark eyes. Aunt Bee would always say she found Amber in the cabbage patch, probably left by fairies.

As we were packing up the car to leave, Amber ran out with a book in her hand. She handed it to me and said, "Write it down. It'll make you feel better." She gave me a big hug that I felt through my whole body. Then she ran back into the house.

I looked at the book she had given me. It was a notebook with a little girl on the front, standing in a field of flowers and wearing a big blue bonnet. When I opened it, it was blank. Just empty, lined pages. Lydia looked over my shoulder. "That's Holly Hobbie," she said. I didn't know who that was. "You should write a story on the way home," Lydia suggested.

As we drove, the thrill of the starry night faded, and the familiar ache for Mom and Wayne returned, tightening its grip on my chest. I opened the notebook. I didn't know how to write about that pain, but I knew I had to start somewhere. My story would be one of triumph over tragedy. I had to believe it.

CHAPTER EIGHT

The Fragile Bubble

Summer ended, and we were back home. Lydia, Marian, Jamie, River, and I arrived with my dad. I didn't know where Wayne was; no one talked about him anymore. I was afraid to ask, wondering if he had died as the Ouija board predicted. Being home with just Dad, and without Mom, felt strange. He seemed like a stranger; I hadn't seen him in a long time. I wanted to go to school and pretend that everything would be okay. Maybe if I pretended enough, it really would be. We had a couple of weeks before school started.

The house was incredibly quiet. I think we all felt the same way. What would happen next?

My dad must have gone to the store before picking us up from Granny's. The fridge was full of food—the fullest I'd seen in a very long time. We had cheese, milk, and he even bought Frosted Flakes. I started to remember that Dad ate Frosted Flakes before bed most nights. I always thought that was funny—breakfast before bed, not in the morning when he woke up. He would say, "Eating breakfast before bed gives me a head start for a new day."

We also had a new color TV, much bigger than the black-and-white one I'd found in his closet and used to watch Billy Graham on Sunday mornings. It had two wire antennas that we had to move around if the picture was static. Dad would say, "Go up there and move the rabbit ears." Then he'd instruct, "No, move them the other way," or "No, put them together," or "Well, maybe spread them apart," then "Wait," and "No, make one shorter and one longer." We would spend thirty minutes finding the clearest picture, and finally, he'd yell, "Stop!" As soon as I stopped and let go, it would go static again, and we'd have to start all over.

We'd finally get a good enough picture for him to watch Captain Kirk in Star Trek or Gunsmoke, or some other boring show no one else liked. Then he would demand that we be quiet while he was watching TV. That's what Dad did most of the time he was home alone with us. He would watch TV and tell us, "Keep it down. I can't hear myself think." I don't know how he could hear himself think with the TV so loud; we couldn't hear each other talk standing side by side.

Often, I would get my drawing pad and pencils and sit beside Dad, drawing while he watched TV. I could be quiet, drawing, and still be with him. I would draw trees, lakes, rivers, and other nature scenes. Most of the time, though, I would draw faces. I especially liked drawing eyes. I really liked drawing all the features of a face—the lips, the nose, the eyebrows. I think I liked capturing expressions and emotions. Sometimes I would just draw different features without actually drawing a face; I would draw several eyes or several mouths. I could sit and draw for hours. It was almost like I disappeared into another realm of reality—one that I created and had control over.

Occasionally, Dad would turn off the TV and play his guitar and sing. I liked it when he would sing. I loved music. It reminded me of warm summer nights in the mountains, catching fireflies with my cousins, listening to the distant music by the campfire. I missed those times already. Dad would play songs by Johnny Cash, Conway Twitty, Elvis, and others. But my favorite was "Last Kiss" by J. Frank Wilson and the Cavaliers.

> *Well, where, oh, where can my baby be?*
> *The Lord took her away from me*
> *She's gone to heaven, so I got to be good*
> *So I can see my baby when I leave this world*

Music had always spoken to me, and it always connected me and my dad. He could play just about any instrument, switching between the guitar, the banjo, the piano, and the harmonica with ease. He had several guitars—two or three acoustic ones and an electric one with an amplifier. He also kept harmonicas scattered in drawers throughout the house.

My dad also loved to draw. He would draw rivers, trees, log cabins, and different forest animals. He was very creative and could make just about anything from just about anything. He once made a miniature log cabin that was about two feet wide and a foot tall, with the most intricate details. The living space focused around a cobblestone fireplace in the center of the main living area. The curtains were made from real fabric, and there was a bearskin rug laid in front of the fireplace. There was a little sofa and chair, a rocking chair that rocked, a dining table with a small china cabinet that had individual pieces of carved wood made to look like china, tiny drinking goblets, and even a chandelier that hung over the table. There was a small candelabra on the mantel with tiny picture frames and hand-painted wall art no bigger than a quarter. Each room was detailed with made beds with pillows and quilts, dressers with mirrors, different floor rugs, and even an odd pair of shoes, a hat on a coat rack, or other garments sprinkled throughout. The lights on the walls and the chandelier were made from Christmas tree lights and could be turned on by a switch outside the house. I often imagined living there.

My dad was creative, artistic, and most definitely crafty. He would make sconces to sell from hardwood like walnut or oak. He would set up sawhorses in the backyard and cut different shapes and sizes to make different styles of sconces. Once they were stained and varnished, he would have me go door to door and sell them throughout our neighborhood. "Okay, you sell these for seven dollars a set, and I will give you a dollar for every set you sell," he'd say.

I would take a sample of each sconce and an order form door to door. I was a pretty good salesperson at eight years old. Some weeks I'd get ten or twelve orders. My dad would say, "It's always good to have a talent for making side money."

It was nice having my dad home.

That brief time with him was a fragile bubble of normalcy, a world contained within our house where creativity was currency and I had a purpose. But the bubble couldn't last. It ended abruptly at the front door. When the first day of school arrived, I stepped out of that sanctuary and into a world that didn't know about miniature log cabins or hand-carved sconces. It was a world that judged based on clothes and lunch tickets, and the safety I had felt just days before vanished completely.

Starting third grade was a big deal for me. Although I had gone to the same school from kindergarten through second grade, it felt like I was entering a whole new school. And I felt like an outcast. From the very first day, it seemed that everyone knew everyone. Friend groups were already formed, and everyone knew which group they fit into. I did not. It became really clear to me during lunchtime.

I stood in line waiting to get my lunch. I could hear the girls behind me talking. "Did you see what she is wearing?" one girl said to the other. "I know, look at her shoes. She must have found them in the dumpster." Another girl a little further away jumped into the conversation. "She has a free lunch ticket. Maybe that's why she can't afford to dress better." They all giggled. I tucked my lunch ticket into my fist.

After the third time I asked someone if I could sit beside them and they said no, I took my lunch to one of the tables lined against the wall where all the extra chairs were stacked and ate alone. A lunch attendant came over. "Why aren't you sitting with the other kids?" she asked.

"I have to study, and it's quiet over here," I replied. She knew I was lying but thankfully walked away. After that, I would grab a small lunch, put it in my backpack, and eat in the bathroom or outside in the doorway by the basketball courts.

We were only a few weeks into the new school year when things changed again.

When I arrived home from school, I noticed a strange car in our driveway. It was a big brown car, stuffed with bags, clothes, and other junk. The license plate said Nebraska.

I went into the house. There was a woman I'd never seen before sitting at our kitchen table. I didn't see my dad or my brothers and sisters.

The heavy octagonal table was tucked tightly in the breakfast nook, too large for the narrow galley kitchen. She sat up straight and tall, wedged between the wall and the table. It was like she was there for a job interview, patiently waiting for her scheduled appointment, tapping her long, hard nails on the table. She was nicely dressed. Her hair was neat, short, and tightly curled. She wore more makeup than my mom and smelled of strong, sweet perfume and cigarette smoke. It was familiar, and it made me feel a little sick. Her nails were long and painted pearl white. She was chewing gum that made a popping sound as she chomped down.

She didn't say anything to me. She just looked at me with her hollow blue eyes. She had painted, narrow lips that smirked between chews. I asked, "Are those your real nails?" She looked at me like I was an idiot. Then she let out what I couldn't tell if it was a huff or a sarcastic chuckle before she spoke. "Uh, of course." This interaction did not make me feel good.

My dad came into the room. "This is Sue. She is our new housekeeper. She has two daughters. They are upstairs with Lydia getting settled in. They are going to be living with us now. Sue is going to help me with you kids when I go back out to sea," he explained in a matter-of-fact tone. My stomach sank.

"You and Marian are going to stay in your room," my dad said. At eight, I was getting too old to share my bed with my little sister. I had hoped I would have my own room soon. "Lydia will be sharing her room with Sue's daughters, Amy and Tammy." I would also occasionally sneak into Lydia's room at night if I got too scared or if I was trying to hide from my nighttime visitor. Now what was I going to do? "Jamie and River will share the other room," he finally finished.

He could see that I was not happy with this news. I didn't ask where Wayne would sleep. I wanted to disappear.

CHAPTER NINE

Remnants of Disillusioned Hope

Today's Lydia's fifteenth birthday. No one knows but me, and she asked me not to tell anyone. I made her a card with birthday candles on it.

Lydia was a year older than Tammy and two years older than Amy, but she seemed twice their age. Lydia had been the only responsible caregiver I had ever had. She took care of me for years, making sure I was clean, safe, and fed as often as possible. Lydia would give anything to me before she took anything for herself. Sometimes it felt like Lydia was the only person who saw me, acknowledged I was there, and would talk to me. Since Sue and her daughters arrived, Lydia had become silent. Tammy and Amy were loud, opinionated, and harsh. They laughed among themselves as if everything was a private joke. The house felt more uncomfortable than ever.

When I wasn't in school, I spent much of my time in my room. I always did my homework. That I could control and excel at. It felt good to be recognized for good grades. Because I didn't have any friends, I focused on getting my work done during the school day. At home, I used homework as an escape from my uncomfortable reality. When I wasn't doing schoolwork, I mostly read and drew.

Sue had each of us do chores on the weekends. She would write out a list of chores with our names beside each and tape it to the refrigerator. I would have to sweep and mop the floors, or do the dishes every night after dinner, or clean the bathrooms. It changed each week.

We were also responsible for keeping our rooms clean and putting our clothes in the laundry for her to wash and dry. We would have to fold them and put them away when they were clean. "I better not find these clean clothes on the floor," she would say. "I spent all day cleaning you kids' clothes." They did smell really good. I couldn't remember them smelling so good before. It felt like magic.

Sue also made sure my clothes were tidy. If they had a tear, she would sew them. She had a big sewing machine that she put on our kitchen table. She could sew really well, making her own clothes from patterns she would buy at the fabric store. Sometimes I would go with her on a Saturday morning. It would get me out of doing my chores for a few hours. Plus, I loved looking at and feeling all the different fabrics and buttons.

Sue would always head straight to the remnant table. "This is where you'll find the biggest deals," she would say. "Patterns are so expensive," she complained as she fumbled through the discount patterns on the table. She held similar McCall and Simplicity mumu dress patterns in each hand, studying them. She would flip them back and forth, over and over, as she dug through the stacks of fabric, comparing the cut size of the fabrics with the pattern requirements.

"Can I help you find anything?" the store clerk asked her. "Is everything on this table 50% off?" Sue asked. "Yes," she replied.

"There's also another remnant table over there," she continued, pointing to the back of the store. Sue walked to the other table and began digging through its contents. I began to wish I had stayed home.

Back home, Sue set up the ironing board and ironed the fabric, removing all the creases. She laid the fabric on the kitchen table and pinned cut portions of the pattern to it. She would follow the pattern and cut each piece, leaving the paper pattern pinned to each cut of fabric. She would put the scraps of extra material in a basket on the floor. "If I collect enough scraps, I can make a quilt," she said. I had hoped for scraps for new Barbie clothes, but I didn't ask. Then, suddenly, Sue remembered I had chores to do and reminded me to get them done.

I slowly crawled up the steps to clean the hall bathroom. I began to think about the light. Maybe just the bathroom light on with the door open would be enough for me to be able to see at night and not be afraid. Maybe I didn't need the hall light on. It had been a long time since I had a nighttime visit. Maybe it was before we went to live with Granny. I wasn't sure if I remembered correctly. Maybe it wouldn't happen anymore, and I could get up to use the bathroom. My thoughts rambled as I scrubbed the base of the toilet. How did this part of the bathroom get so dirty? You can't even walk here!

I caught a glimpse of River sitting cross-legged just outside the bathroom door as I peeked through the hole under the toilet bowl. He was wearing a dirty pair of tan shorts and nothing else. He had dry dirt caked down each side of his chest that stuck to whatever sticky juice he'd let run down his body hours ago. He was playing with his toes with one hand, and the other was in his mouth as he often chewed on his fingers. Drool was adding moisture to the center of his chest, creating a shiny, clear area.

"Whatcha doin'?" he said with a sloppy, wet, fist-in-mouth smile.

"I'm looking for fairies," I said. "I found some troll poop back here. I know trolls eat fairies, so I'm looking for their hiding spot," I carried on. "I thought I saw one run back here when I swept the floor. Come look!"

River jumped up and ran over to the toilet. "Where? Where? I don't see nuffin!" he said. "You have to look closer," I encouraged. River bent over so far his stringy blonde hair dipped slightly in the toilet bowl. "Lemme seeee!" he was getting louder. I couldn't help but laugh. It felt good to laugh.

Just then, Sue was standing angrily in the doorway. "Why are you playing and not doing your chores?" she said through clenched teeth. "River? Is your hair wet? Did you stick your head in the toilet?!" she yelled, yanking River up off the ground by his armpit. She slapped him across the back of his head. It was a loud, hard slap. He instantly began crying.

"That's disgusting! Get in the other bathroom and get in the tub!" she yelled as she tossed him onto the floor like a dirty, wet towel. "Lydia! Lydia!" she screamed down the hall. I heard Lydia in the distance, "Yeah?" "Don't 'yeah' me," Sue raged. "Get in there and give your filthy brother a bath. You know he put his head in the toilet?!" I saw Lydia skulk behind Sue, heading to the other bathroom.

"As for you, young lady," she turned her anger towards me. "As soon as you're done, I want you in bed." It was still light out and nowhere near getting dark. "What about dinner?" I asked. "Do you really think you deserve dinner after putting your brother's head in the toilet?!" I hadn't eaten lunch because I went to the fabric store with her earlier, and I was really hungry. I started to say something as she began to walk away. She briskly turned her head back to me and glared into my soul, almost daring me to speak. I went silent. She stormed away, and I soon heard her in the other bathroom yelling at River and Lydia. Both of them were now crying.

I lay in bed, witnessing the light turning to a purplish, hazy dusk, then finally a deep darkness. I thought about how I made River get in trouble and how Lydia was always responsible for us. I thought about my dad and became so mad at him for always leaving us. I hated Sue. She hated laughter because she hated life. Of this, I was sure. I thought about my Granny, the farm, my cousins, how I loved to be dirty and free. Freedom was so distant from here. After hours of mind tangles, I drifted off to sleep.

I was awoken by the need to pee. I felt like my stomach was going to explode. The hall light was off. It was dark. But I convinced myself that nothing had happened in a long time. Sue was there, and everyone was afraid of her. Nothing would happen if I got up and went to pee. I took the chance. I tiptoed as quietly as I could. I could hear Sue snoring loudly as I passed her closed bedroom door, the same bedroom that had been my mom and dad's before. I quietly returned to bed and pulled the covers up over my head. "Okay, now disappear," I told myself over and over.

It didn't work. Shortly after I returned to bed, I realized that I was not alone. It hadn't stopped. I was wrong. At eight years old, I truly wanted to die.

Marian's cries and screams pierce the morning silence again. "Kathy peed the bed! I'm all wet!"

I get up and begin cleaning, soaking up urine with bath towels. Sue's heavy footsteps on the stairs shake the walls, dislodging one of my drawings tacked above the dresser. I watch it fall in slow motion to the floor. At the same moment, Sue steps into my room, her foot landing directly on it. She doesn't even acknowledge the paper, crushing and ripping it as she lunges toward me.

I look up from her feet to see a thick, black men's belt in her hand— my dad's belt. He just returned home a few days ago. She grabs me by the arm and throws me facedown onto the urine-soaked bed. She begins beating me, screaming, "Why do you keep pissing in the bed? Do you know how nasty that is? Poor Marian has to wake up every day in pee because her big sister won't get up to go to the bathroom. How lazy are you?"

I cry and beg her to stop, but she doesn't want an answer. She is angry. "Do you think I like washing pissy sheets every day of my life?" With each question, she welts my backside. Sometimes the strap hits higher on my back, and it feels like a sword has just slashed me.

After what seems like an eternity, I hear my dad come up the steps. "Alright, I think that's enough," he says to Sue.

Out of breath now, she turns and storms out of the room. "You deal with your nasty daughter then," she says, her voice trailing down the hall.

"Alright now, get up and get yourself cleaned up," he says, his voice weak. "You need to listen to your mother so this doesn't happen again."

My mother? This horrible woman is not my mother. My real mother is gone. She left me here and doesn't care if some other woman comes in and beats me. And I guess, neither does he.

I can't say this, though. I can barely breathe, sobbing so hard. I can't tell him that I'm terrified to get up in the middle of the night. I can't tell him I'm just a kid and can't hold my bladder for so long.

"Go wash your face and bring those dirty sheets down here," Sue yells up the stairs. "I don't want to look at that bawling face."

I sit on the floor for the longest time. Marian comes over, puts her hand on my shoulder, and says, "I'm sorry I got you a spanking." I don't move. I don't want Marian's apology.

Later that afternoon, my dad says, "Let's go for a ride." I'm the only one Dad takes on his motorcycle. He says it's because I'm the only one who doesn't throw off his balance. I'm just happy for the escape.

I grab my giant metallic green helmet. It's huge on my head, but my dad pulls the straps extra tight until it doesn't move. I get on the back of the motorcycle behind him, holding tight around his waist. He always says the same thing as we take off: "Hold on!"

Being on the back of the motorcycle makes me feel free, like a bird soaring through the sky. I pretend that I have wings and can fly anywhere. We ride for a long time down winding roads with trees lining the sides, creating a tunnel of branches and leaves. The light flickers between them as we pass through, reminding me of the disco lights I've seen on American Bandstand.

We stop at a little diner called Monks. "What would you like to drink, sweetie?" the lady behind the counter asks.

"I'll have a Dr. Pepper, please," I reply. She pops open a cold can and slides it across the counter to me. The outside of the can is wet, with drips of condensation running down its sides. I can hear the bubbles fizzing. I'm not only thirsty, but hungry too. After the beating, Sue decided she didn't want to look at me, which meant she didn't feed me.

"Hungry?" my dad asks.

"Yes," I say, not looking up from my Dr. Pepper.

"We'll have two cheeseburgers and fries," my dad tells the lady.

"You want everything on it?" she asks. My dad looks at me, and I nod. "Yup, load it up," he says.

She turns to the man at the grill. "Two cheeseburgers with everything and fries." He raises his chin in acknowledgment and keeps cooking. I watch as he grabs a huge handful of raw hamburger, rolls it into a ball, and then smashes it onto the hot, flat iron grill. It sizzles loud. The grill is already filled with burgers. Some have cheese, and some don't. Just before putting a burger on a bun, he toasts the bun on the grill.

Within minutes, the lady sets two plates with stacked cheeseburgers and fries in front of us. She grabs the ketchup from a metal bin and places it between our plates. "You guys need anything else?" she asks.

"Not right now. I think we're good," my dad says, smiling at me. He knows I'm starving.

The burgers are loaded. They have tomatoes, lettuce, onions, mayo, ketchup, pickles, and mustard. When I try to take a bite, a mixture of condiments and mushy tomatoes pours out the back of the bun, down my fingers, and onto the plate as I squish it into my mouth. It is the best cheeseburger I have ever eaten.

When my tummy is full, we get back on the motorcycle and ride to Stumpy Lake. It is beautiful there, so peaceful. Giant green lily pads cover the water in patches with delicate, pointed pink flowers floating atop them. There are so many dragonflies I lose count. We stay for just a few minutes before my dad says, "Well, we'd better be getting home. I'm sure Sue is wondering where we got off to."

I don't care if Sue is wondering. I don't want to leave. I never want to go back home.

Shortly after my dad left again and went back out to sea. Leaving us with Sue.

CHAPTER TEN

Promises and Strangers

Although my mother was eventually found, we never went back to living with her. Occasionally, she would pick us up, and we'd spend a couple of hours with her. She'd take us to a local pool hall to drink beer and smoke while we played with the balls on the pool table. She always had smelly friends who would offer us change for the jukebox.

"Here you go, hun," a man with no front teeth and bad breath said as he handed me a coin, his words slurring out in a slow, wet drawl. "Go pick a song on the jukebox for us."

Marian and River loved the attention, but I never felt comfortable with the strangers my mother surrounded herself with. Like Lydia, I was just waiting for her to disappear again—for things to go back to the way they had been.

After several of these short visits over a few months, my dad agreed to let us spend the weekend with her. I was actually excited. I got up really early that Saturday morning and put on my favorite Sunday school dress—a soft yellow one with a big bow at the waist. I wore my patent leather shoes, which were actually plastic, and white socks folded down with a lace trim. In my small, round suitcase from Christmas, the one with brightly colored dancing teddy bears on the front, I packed a pair of pants, a shirt, underwear, socks, tennis shoes, and pajamas. I brushed my hair 100 times, just as Lydia had told me: "You have to brush your hair 100 strokes for it to stay shiny and strong." I was ready. I pictured her braiding my hair in the morning, or maybe she'd take us to the beach. I imagined her smiling, looking at me the way the mothers on TV looked at their daughters.

I remember so clearly the narrow window that ran alongside the front door. I pulled a kitchen chair over, set my suitcase down, and sat watching for my mother to arrive. I sat, and I waited.

Sue brought me a peanut butter and jelly sandwich. "I know you must be getting hungry," she said.

"Thank you," I replied, careful not to get anything on my dress.

Hours seemed to pass. I listened to the hum of the refrigerator and the distant ticking of the grandfather clock in the hall. Each tick felt like an hour. My legs grew numb. With every car that drove by, I stretched to see the driver, a small tingle of hope rising in my belly only to be replaced by a deep, sinking feeling as it passed.

The day was long.

Finally, Sue came over and placed her hand on my shoulder. I didn't need her to say it. A cold, heavy knowing had already settled in my stomach an hour earlier, but I had refused to listen to it. I looked up, bracing myself for the inevitable. "She's not coming, honey," she said in a soft, compassionate voice. It was the first time I had ever felt any kindness from her, and yet her words felt like a blade slowly piercing my spirit. A single tear rolled down my face. I picked up my suitcase and walked slowly up the stairs to my room.

In that moment, I swore I would never be like my mother. I would never disappoint anyone the way she had just disappointed me. My mind played the same question on a loop: Why didn't she love me?

The fragile truce that had formed between Sue and me that afternoon shattered as quickly as it had appeared. The house settled back into its familiar, tense silence, but the silence inside of me was louder than ever. I retreated further into myself, spending my time drawing in my Holly Hobbie notebook. I filled its pages not with stories, but with faces—eyes that held sadness, mouths that couldn't speak. My real mother was a ghost, and my real granny was a distant memory. I was a daughter without a mother, a granddaughter without a grandmother. I didn't realize it then, but I was searching for a replacement, for any figure who could fill the aching void she had left.

It was against this backdrop of quiet desperation that I found myself one evening sitting quietly on the sofa, my notebook open on my lap, drawing trees and remembering the ones at my granny's house. I closed my eyes and let my mind wander, imagining I was one of them, rooted deeply in the earth. I could almost smell the apples on the hill and feel the warm sun on my branches, a part of the soil once again.

Here in the living room, the air felt stagnant, heavy with the smell of old smoke. The television blared, its sound deafening. Dad was in his recliner, and Sue was beside him in a rocking chair, a quiet click-clack accompanying the smacking of chewing gum between her teeth. An embroidery ring was in her hand, tiny flowers taking shape with each stitch as she watched the evening news.

"President Ronald Reagan has signed the Omnibus Budget Reconciliation Act, significantly cutting Medicaid," the reporter announced. "Many local nursing homes are being forced to release residents... Some are likely to end up homeless as they no longer have family support."

Sue's stitching stopped. "We need to do something," she said, her voice low. "They can't just release these poor people with nowhere to go."

A couple of weeks later, Dad and Sue came home with an elderly woman. She carried two large suitcases, which I assumed held all of her worldly possessions.

"This is Mrs. McCade," Sue explained. "We've adopted her as your new grandmother. She's going to be staying with us from now on. You can call her Grandma McCade."

The words hung in the stale, smoky air. I looked at my dad, my breath held tight, waiting for him to correct her. He was our dad; he was supposed to be the one who decided. But he just looked at Sue, then at the floor, and nodded once, as if agreeing to the weather. The breath I was holding escaped in a cold, hollow rush.

Grandma McCade was thin and frail, a stark contrast to my own granny, who was plump and full of life. Her huge, round glasses seemed to swallow her narrow, pale face, making her small blue eyes appear even deeper. Her thin white hair attempted to curl but was too short. Her shoulders were slumped, her back hunched beneath a tattered white cardigan that buttoned tightly at her neck. A handkerchief with a tiny embroidered rose hung from one sleeve, and a string of black beads with a small cross wrapped around the other wrist. She smelled of a damp, musky sweetness that reminded me of old roses that had begun to wilt and lose their petals.

She offered a narrow, timid smile. "Hello," she said softly, in an accent I hadn't heard before.

Sue told us that Grandma McCade's family lived in New York and that her son didn't have the space to take her in. I couldn't help but wonder how our small, four-bedroom townhouse had room when his home didn't, especially with seven kids already living with us. We still had to ration what we had with so many mouths to feed, and now we were adding one more.

I looked at this frail woman with her whole life in two suitcases and felt a pang of pity, but it was quickly followed by something else: the cold dread of another ghost in our house, living or otherwise.

Because Grandma McCade used a walker and couldn't climb the stairs, the living room became her bedroom. She slept in Dad's recliner, her suitcases stacked neatly behind it—a constant reminder of her impermanence. We were told to be quiet on the stairs and weren't allowed in the living room when she was asleep, which was most of the time.

Sometimes, if the stars aligned and Sue was feeling generous, she would allow me the privilege of joining her and her daughters to watch General Hospital. The familiar, crackling theme music would fill the room as they gathered, their eyes wide with a desperate eagerness, hungering to devour every twist and turn of Luke and Laura's tumultuous lives. For them, it was the raw drama, the passionate declarations, and the heart-wrenching betrayals that captivated them. They dissected every glance and whispered word with the intensity of forensic scientists, their emotions mirroring the on-screen melodrama.

I, however, found myself less enthralled by the romance. While I appreciated the escapism, my true focus was on something more fundamental: the simple, profound act of belonging. To be included in their huddle, to be one of them in that moment, was a balm to my often-solitary spirit. Participating in their animated conversations about this fantastical world created a tangible link between us. In those shared moments, discussing the latest cliffhanger or a character's questionable decision, I felt less alone. It was as if, for that one hour, we were all taking a collective breath, escaping our individual worlds to find common ground.

During the weekends, Sue insisted we stay outside until the streetlights came on, punishing us if we came inside for any reason. My routine was a solitary one. I found sanctuary in the neighborhood park, always in the same spot: a large concrete tunnel. It was cool and echoing, a haven from the outside world where I was content in my own company, the quiet hum of my thoughts a constant companion. The tunnel, with its rough, gray walls, offered a peculiar comfort, a sense of enclosure that felt both protective and isolated. It was a place where I could be a silent witness to the ebb and flow of park life while remaining firmly on the periphery.

It was a Saturday afternoon. Sue must have gone to the store; I didn't see her car. Thirsty and bored after hours at the park, I decided to slip inside for a quick drink, thinking Sue wouldn't know.

The moment I stepped through the door, I saw her, gripping her walker. She turned and yelled, "What are you doing in the house?" I had never seen her angry. "Did you come in here to check up on me?" she demanded, her voice sharp. "I can get up and walk around if I want to. I don't need some kid checking up on me," she muttered. In that moment, she reminded me of Sue—just plain mean. I felt terrible and instantly knew I was in trouble.

"I was just getting a drink of water," I tried to explain, but she didn't want to hear it, waving her hand at me in a clear 'get out' gesture.

I understood then that Sue could never truly be my mother, despite my dad's insistence, just as Grandma McCade would never be my grandmother. This only deepened my longing for my real mom and Granny, whose memories began to fade as the days dragged on. Sue and Grandma McCade quickly clashed. Soon, Sue informed us that Grandma McCade's medical needs had become too demanding and returned her to the nursing home.

A few months later, Sue told us of Grandma McCade's passing. Her son had her body returned to New York. We never saw her again. Now, she was gone forever. I wondered if we would adopt another grandmother.

Ghosts were a common, openly discussed presence in my family. Shortly after Grandma McCade's passing, she appeared to me. I was just waking, my eyes half-closed, when I saw her in the doorway. She was without her walker, her face a creamy pink, radiating health and happiness. Her back was straight. She walked effortlessly to my bed, sat beside me, and took my hand. It was warm, impossibly so, chasing the chill from my bones as she gently rubbed the back of it as she smiled. I closed my eyes, fighting back tears. When I opened them, she was gone.

It was still very early. Dad was gone, and Sue was still asleep. I went into her room. "Grandma McCade just came into my room, sat on my bed, and held my hand," I said, my voice trembling.

"That was her way of telling you she was okay," Sue replied without hesitation.

It meant a lot that Sue didn't dismiss what I had told her. In that moment, she had confirmed one of my deepest truths: at twelve years old, I knew I could see and communicate with the dead.

PART III

The Alchemy

The events of the past are never truly behind us; they are the soil from which our future grows. You have witnessed the trauma and the search for safety. Now, you will see how the scars became a map, and the coping mechanisms became a key. This is the story of the alchemy itself—the conscious act of turning the deepest wounds into a sacred gift.

CHAPTER ELEVEN

Finding My Own Way

The saying "time heals all wounds" was never true for me. Time didn't heal; it only buried my pain deeper. With each passing year, I drifted from the little girl I once was until she became a stranger. My teenage years were a desperate attempt to numb the feelings of being invisible and worthless—of being discarded once my usefulness expired. I experimented with drugs, alcohol, and reckless behaviors that could have easily ended my life. Since no one seemed to care about me, I stopped caring about myself, and the chasm between who I was and that lost little girl widened.

Most people search for the safety they knew as a child. I had no such place to return to. My "known world" was chaos, so chaos was what I sought out. I found it in boys with distant eyes and fast cars, in relationships destined to end before they even began. Quiet stability felt foreign and threatening; I chose the familiar storm, confusing the need to protect myself with love. It was a self-fulfilling prophecy: if I chose people who would eventually leave, I would never be surprised by the pain of abandonment. I was in control of my own destruction.

This pattern was never clearer than on the nights I found myself walking alone through Hollywood Cemetery in Richmond, Virginia. At 2:00 a.m., I would wander the dark paths in one of the highest crime areas in the country, daring fate to show me something scarier than what I had already survived.

"Come get me!" I screamed silently to the dark.

This disassociation was shaping my future, forging habits rooted in a deep-seated fear of abandonment and rejection. I was developing new ways to protect myself, piling them on top of the defenses I'd built as a child. Growing up, my intuition had been my guide. I developed a sharp sense of telepathy to anticipate danger and stay safe, learning to "hear" what people were thinking by being still, allowing their thoughts to become louder than my own. To protect myself, I learned to step back and let other personalities emerge. It was all for survival.

By my senior year, I had found healthier ways to cope. My boyfriend, who was planning to attend art college, encouraged me to consider it as well. I loved creating art and saw a potential career. I also had a job, which gave me my own money and a sense of independence. At seventeen, I was almost fully self-sufficient—buying my own clothes, car, and insurance. I spent as little time at my parents' house as possible, leaving the drugs and alcohol behind to focus on college, on escaping as far as I could from the place that had stolen my childhood.

"What makes you think you're better than your brothers and sisters? We can't afford to send you to college. You should just get a job at McDonald's," my stepmother, Sue, would say. By the time I left, I had been hearing her voice for nearly a decade. It stayed with me, constantly chipping away at my confidence, yet it also became a powerful driving force—a burning desire to prove her wrong. Her world was small and full of pain, but I knew I was destined for something more.

Because my family was poor, I was able to go to college using Pell Grants, student loans, and work-study. I enrolled at Virginia Commonwealth University, two hours away from Virginia Beach. I moved away from my childhood home and never returned. It was the escape that shaped my entire life, finally allowing me to build a new foundation.

Sue visited me once at VCU. We toured the campus, and for the first time, I felt a small glimmer of pride from her. Shortly after, I learned she had left my dad. She packed up in the middle of the night and moved to Nebraska. I never saw or spoke to her again.

I learned of her death several years later.

Aftermath

My siblings experienced their own traumas. Wayne finally reappeared after several years with a wife and a baby. We learned later that after the Ouija board incident, terrified that he was marked for death, he had run from the house that day and never stopped running. That fear pushed him onto the streets, where survival meant something else entirely. He was picked up for shoplifting—not for thrills, but just to feed himself—and spent years in and out of juvenile detention. No one ever looked for him; no one ever looked out for Wayne. He eventually found his way into a jobs program in another state, but his was a different kind of survival story, one of unspoken ghosts that he never fully shared with any of us.

I was never again close to any of my siblings. They all moved far away and created their own families. As adults, we have very little in common, and I believe we chose to keep that distance because it allows us to distance ourselves from that life.

I spoke to Lydia on the phone not long ago, after she'd heard about my angel portraits. There was a long silence after I tried to explain what I do. "It makes sense," she finally said. "I always remember you being somewhere else, even when you were sitting right there in the room with me."

I asked her what she meant.

"You weren't just quiet, Kathy," she said. "You were listening. To everything. The things people weren't even saying."

In that moment, my childhood protector, without knowing it, had validated my entire life. She saw me using the gift I didn't yet have a name for.

CHAPTER TWELVE

Sanctuary in the Dark

My husband sleeps with two of the flattest pillows I've ever seen. I often joke with him and say, "Why do you even bother sleeping with pillows at all?"

On the other hand, I spend the entire night shuffling five pillows of various sizes and firmness.

We start our nightly routine early, typically around 8:30 PM. He is required to be at work at 5:45 AM. After 30 years of marriage, I've become accustomed to sharing his sleep schedule. I go to bed early and, almost every night, I wake up in the middle of the night.

This has become my witching hour. In college, I recall that time being about the same, around 2:00–3:00 AM. Except back then, I would typically go to bed afterwards. During this finite period of time, I find myself to be more creative, more artistic, more focused, and probably the most productive I am in any 24-hour period. Sometimes I will get up and work on projects for my day job. Other times I will write, draw, paint, or simply meditate. Whatever I do, this time is mine and mine alone.

Each night we climb into bed together around 8:30. Then, we spend about an hour together as we each fall asleep. He typically watches TV or plays games on his phone while I read or listen to podcasts with my headphones on.

We start out the night with our three dogs in bed with us. Our yellow lab Ginger, Zeus our black pug, and Luna our miniature Chihuahua. Ginger lies between my husband and me, stretching the entire length of the bed. Zeus curls up under my feet. And Luna finds refuge where she can under the blankets. Sometime after we fall asleep, both Ginger and Luna retire to their respective dog beds on opposite sides of the room. Zeus spends the night in and out of the blankets as he gets hot and cold.

I stack my five pillows behind me: two heavier, feather pillows on the bottom, and I build a pyramid of progressively fluffier and lighter pillows on top. I use this as my backrest as I sink into a reclining position. I pull the weighted down duvet covers up to my chest and tighten them around me like a cocoon.

I am fully aware that five pillows offer no real defense against a human threat. It's an illusion of safety, a child's logic playing out in an adult's bed. But the ritual itself is the point. It's a physical manifestation of a promise I'm making to that little girl—a promise that tonight, I am the one in control, I am the one building the walls.

As I drift off, I often find myself rubbing my feet together. I recently learned this can be an unconscious trauma response. When I consider my entire sleep routine, it's clear that much of it might be a reflection of that same unconscious response.

As a child, I never felt safe. I never felt protected. Not even in bed. Especially not in bed.

I would go to bed early and then be awoken in the middle of the night, typically around 2:00–3:00 AM. During this time, my innocence as a child was lost. My body was violated, and there was no one and nothing that protected me in those moments.

I'm not sure at what age the abuse started or how old I was when it stopped. I just remember that time as ascending from my body, disconnected from the action of the nightly routine. For years it continued. For years I disappeared, disassociated from my body.

Today, 50 years later, I find myself building a fortress around my body each night.

When I transition from reclining to sleeping, there are two very conscious considerations I employ when constructing my fortress—my comfort level and my level of protection.

I use one of the two heavy down pillows as a base for my head. Lying on my right side, facing away from my husband, I place a lighter, fluffy pillow at a 45-degree angle under my face. The other heavy down pillow is placed between my bent knees. The other two fluffy pillows get securely tucked behind and in front of me as I snuggle up tightly in the fetal position.

An illusion of safety and protection created nightly.

The dark, quiet hours of my witching hour are a stark contrast to those terrifying nights of my childhood. Then, the darkness held the promise of violation, a terror I endured alone. Now, it offers a sanctuary, a canvas for creativity, a space where I can reclaim myself. The same stillness I once used to listen for footsteps in the hall, I now use to listen for inspiration. The hyper-awareness that was once a tool for survival has been transmuted into a channel for creativity. The darkness that once held only fear now holds a quiet, creative power that is mine and mine alone.

I may still build my pillow fortresses, a physical manifestation of a lifelong need for safety, but within those walls, I am no longer lost. I am present, I am creating, I am healing. The scars are there, etched into my memory, but they no longer define me.

My husband loves to tell the story of the night he thought I was possessed. We were young, still in that fragile, early stage of dating where you're learning each other's landscapes. I was asleep, lying on my side with my back to him, when he apparently heard a strange sound. Curious, he simply lifted himself up to peer over my shoulder. He didn't touch me, didn't make a sound.

But the moment his face entered my space, my eyes shot wide open. I let out what he describes as the deepest, most soul-shaking gasp he'd ever heard. It was pure, instinctual terror. He bolted out of bed as if launched, screaming, "What the hell, Kathy?!" in sheer panic.

Once he'd recovered from his "near-death experience," the tension shattered, and we both collapsed in a fit of hysterical laughter that melted into tears. To this day, he recounts that night with increasingly dramatic flair. "It was a true Exorcist moment," he'll tell our friends, his eyes wide. "Her head spun almost all the way around, and I was convinced she was possessed!" We all roar with laughter every time.

Poor guy, so young and naive, he had no idea what he was signing up for. But that night, he didn't just see a strange, terrified reaction; he saw a glimpse of the wound beneath it. And he stayed. In a life where so many people had been a source of danger, his laughter, his refusal to be scared away, became its own kind of sanctuary.

It turns out that night wasn't an isolated incident. Over the years, I've had similar reactions when sleeping with girlfriends or sharing hotel rooms. Innocent gestures from others, like looking at me or whispering my name, have triggered the same terrified response. Consequently, I've had to establish some strict rules for anyone I sleep near. I preface them with the story of nearly giving my husband a heart attack.

"You absolutely cannot stare at me while I'm asleep, not for any amount of time," I tell them. "It doesn't matter how far away you are. Just don't look at me." I chuckle as I explain, "My automatic response will always be to sit straight up in bed, eyes popping wide open, gasping for dear life." I continue, "This also applies if you stand next to the bed or whisper my name. Just don't do it."

I never delve into the childhood trauma that causes this unique reaction. Interestingly, I've also never had this response when my children wake me up in the middle of the night. It seems to be reserved exclusively for other adults. I've often wondered about this exemption. Perhaps a mother's protective instinct is simply a more powerful frequency, one that overrides the static of old trauma. My body's alarm system was built to detect a specific kind of adult threat. My children were never that. They were inherently safe, the ones I was shielding, not the ones I needed shielding from. My soul just knew the difference.

I've spent a lifetime doing healing work in the light to release the trauma of childhood sexual abuse, of facing the scars of neglect and accepting abandonment. Yet I'm still protecting that little girl who disappeared in the darkest hours.

CHAPTER THIRTEEN

My Angel Portraits

Throughout my childhood, I hid behind a sketchbook. It was a sanctuary built of paper and graphite, a quiet world I could control when the one outside was in chaos. In college, I explored new mediums, but my soul always came back to the simple honesty of a pencil. I loved the feeling of shaping the graphite, the pressure of my hand on the paper creating a life where there was none before.

Art was my first psychic language—an unconscious ability to connect to a higher realm and channel the energy of a different reality. For years, I focused on drawing faces. I was obsessed with capturing the spirit in the eyes, the story in an expression. I loved the stark contrast of the graphite against the crisp white paper, always leaving the backgrounds empty, a void of pure light beyond their faces. After each drawing was complete, I would spray it with fixative and carefully place it in a large art portfolio. For years, a silent congregation of souls lived under my bed, hidden in the dark. They were my witnesses, the only ones who had seen the quiet, interior world of a little girl who so often felt invisible.

Life moved on. At twenty-three, I gave birth to twin boys and married their father. I started a career, built a home, and for a decade, I let life take the reins. On the surface, my life looked like a success. Always an overachiever, I was constantly striving for the next promotion, adding certifications to my resume. My psychic instincts remained my secret navigator, helping me read people and become a strong communications leader. This dive into the psychology of marketing was just another unnamed extension of my abilities. They were powerful, but I hadn't yet acknowledged them as psychic, nor had I associated them with the trauma that had forged them.

But beneath the surface of my achievements, a quiet, relentless question hummed: Is this all there is? It was, I know now, the deep yearning of that little girl I had left behind, still waiting to be truly seen.

I remember the exact moment everything shifted. It happened on a four-hour drive to the mountains for my aunt's funeral, the familiar, melancholic comfort of the Blue Ridge blurring past the window in the rain. As my husband drove, I sketched. But this time, it was different. My hand began to move not with the precision I usually employed, but with a flowing, surrendered grace. An angel began to emerge from my pencil—an elongated, mystical form with wings that seemed to stretch beyond the page. The focus wasn't on meticulous detail, but on its ethereal, spiritual essence. It was a drawing of a feeling, a prayer made of graphite.

After returning home, the weight of my aunt's death left me feeling empty and untethered. I found myself standing in my office, face-to-face with the many portraits I had drawn over the years. My husband had insisted I pull them out from under the bed, frame them, and hang them on the walls. Before, they were just drawings. But now, standing in that room with their eyes on me, I felt a deep sense of belonging. I had unknowingly created a circle of protecting spirits. For the first time, I truly saw them for what they were. It wasn't a choice; it was a command from my soul. One by one, I pulled the drawings off the wall. It was a ritual. With each pencil stroke, I was not just adding wings; I was setting them free. And in freeing them, I was freeing myself. When I was done, I stood in a room surrounded by angels.

That week, I applied to a local art show, Artisans in the Park. My application was accepted. I bought a white tent and heavy gridwall panels, my marketing skills shining as I created a professional display. The day of the show, I walked out onto an empty field marked with white paint, joining the gypsy community of artists as we magically created a city of tents. The air smelled of damp grass and canvas, filled with the cacophony of hammers and hopeful chatter. I felt like a fraud waiting to be discovered, an imposter among these true artisans.

When the show started, I sat in a chair just outside my tent, a knot of fear and hope tangled in my stomach, peeking through a small gap in the side wall. It felt like I was eight years old again, hiding in a doorway, watching the world without being a part of it. To my surprise, people began to come in. They didn't just look; they connected.

"This angel looks exactly like my mother," one woman said with a gasp, her hand flying to her mouth. Tears welled in her eyes. "These are her green eyes." Although my angels were drawn in graphite, I had colored each pair of eyes with brilliant pastels.

An older man stood for a long time in front of an angel with a kind, weathered face. "That's my dad," he said, his voice thick with emotion. "He had that same mischievous look in his eye." He bought the print, telling me he was going to hang it where he could see it every morning.

Another woman walked directly to a drawing of a baby angel held between two hands. She shared that her husband and son were killed in a car accident years ago, and this angel reminded her of them. "See," she said, opening a locket to reveal a photo of her husband holding their smiling baby.

Soon, I was in constant dialogue with visitors who shared tears born from a divine connection. It was a humbling, holy experience. I've often wondered if, in creating these portraits, I had really been channeling spirits for their loved ones to find in my booth that day. I won Best in Show that weekend.

At the next show, a woman approached me. "Have you ever done a commission?" she asked. Her friend had lost a daughter to SIDS, and the anniversary was approaching. She wanted to give her a baby angel portrait. "I would be honored," I said.

The morning the woman was scheduled to pick up the portrait, I was at my office, going through the mundane ritual of unpacking my briefcase. As I did, an intense conversation began streaming through my consciousness—a message for the baby's mother, expressing the profound honor I felt. In the middle of this silent, holy dialogue, something caught my eye. At first, I thought it was a speck of dust, but it didn't float; it moved as if it were alive. It wasn't a gnat; it was silver, shiny... and then it twinkled. The air grew still. A single, silent star had been born in my office.

I was hit with a wave of the most profound humility, gratitude, and grace I have ever known. And then it was gone. I knew, with every fiber of my being, that the spirit of that baby angel had come to thank me. After the portrait was picked up, I sat alone, the feeling of grace still lingering in the air. The thought of putting a price on that experience felt like a betrayal. How could I charge a fee for delivering a message from heaven? How could I commercialize a gift that had been forged in my own silent suffering? It was then I knew: these portraits were not a business. They were a calling. The healing had to be given as freely as the gift was given to me.

After that, I began to draw Angel Memorial Portraits for people all over the world. Throughout the process, I was in constant contact with the soul I was drawing. A little boy once insisted on how his hair needed to look. "My bangs need to be really straight," he told me. "And I want my wings to go straight up and down." I later learned from his mother that he was an artist and had been killed by a freak accident when an airsoft pellet struck his heart.

With every portrait, a piece of my own fractured childhood was healed. In drawing a child who was loved and missed so dearly, I was, in a way, re-parenting the little girl inside me who had felt so unseen. In giving another mother a tangible connection to her child in spirit, I was mending the severed maternal bond within my own soul. I was no longer the invisible girl hiding behind a sketchbook; I was a conduit for a love so powerful it transcended death itself.

That healing also changed my relationship with the past. I saw my father a few years before he passed away. He was older, quieter, and the sharp edges of his memory had softened. We never had a grand confrontation; the time for that was gone. Instead, I showed him one of my angel portraits. He held it with his familiar, crafty hands and traced the outline of a wing. "You always were good at drawing," he said, his voice raspy. "Got that from me."

"I had to find a way to make sense of things," I told him.

He looked at me, a flicker of something—regret, understanding?—in his dark eyes. In that quiet moment, I realized I no longer needed an apology. I had come to see him not as the man who failed to protect me, but as a man who gave me his love for art, a man who was as broken as the rest of us. That acceptance was its own kind of peace.

I later read Wayne Dyer's words, "When you do something in virtue and service, you get the attention of the angelics." I believe my Angel Portraits served as the portal to unlocking my complete potential as a psychic medium. Offering my gifts to the world, with virtue and in service, drew the attention of the celestial realm, which then fully supported my abilities.

PART IV

The Alchemist's Toolkit

You have now walked with me through the darkest parts of my past and witnessed the alchemy that turned that pain into a sacred gift. Now, I want to give you the tools and tactics to begin your own journey of transformation.

CHAPTER FOURTEEN

The First Sanctuary:
Finding Stillness in the Storm

Before we learn to hear the whispers of spirit, before we explore the four clairs, before we even consider opening the channel to the world beyond, we must first learn to do one thing: be still.

I know that for many of you reading this, the word "meditation" lands with the weight of a heavy stone. It conjures images of silent monks on mountaintops, legs folded in impossible positions, minds blissfully empty. It can feel like an insurmountable goal, another thing to fail at, especially when your mind is a storm-tossed sea of anxiety, to-do lists, and the relentless echoes of the past. For those of us whose nervous systems were forged in chaos, the command to "just clear your mind" is not only unhelpful; it can feel like a cruel joke.

So, let us begin by releasing that image. Let us burn it on a ceremonial pyre and scatter the ashes. The journey we are about to embark upon does not begin with an empty mind. It begins with a safe one.

For the intuitive soul shaped by trauma, meditation is not

about achieving emptiness. It is about creating a sanctuary. It is the conscious, intentional act of building a quiet, protected room inside yourself, a place where the frantic watchman in your mind's watchtower can finally come down, have a cup of tea, and know that for this moment, in this breath, all is well. It is any practice that gently brings your awareness to a single point of focus, allowing the chaotic noise of your hyper-vigilant mind to soften, even for a moment, so that another, quieter voice can be heard.

I did not know it at the time, but I have been meditating my entire life. I had to. It was the only way I survived. My first sanctuaries were not built of silence and stillness, but of paper and graphite, of imagination and escape. They were the tools an inventive little girl used to find a moment of peace in a world that offered none.

My sketchbook was my first temple. I can still feel the profound relief that would wash over me as I opened its pages. It was a world I could control. Outside its covers, my life was a chaotic swirl of unpredictable adults, of unspoken tensions and tangible threats. But inside, I was the creator. I was sovereign. The ritual itself was a meditation. I would choose a pencil, feel its familiar weight in my hand, and touch its sharpened point to the crisp, clean paper. In that moment of contact, the noisy, dangerous world would begin to recede.

My focus would narrow to a single point: the place where graphite met paper. I would become lost in the act of creation, in the pressure of my hand shaping a cheekbone, in the delicate dance of my fingers smudging a shadow to create depth. I was obsessed with drawing eyes, with capturing the spirit within them. As I focused on the curve of an eyelid or the tiny flecks of light in a pupil, my own breathing would slow. The frantic buzz of my amygdala would quiet. For those precious hours, I was not a terrified child waiting for the next disaster; I was an artist, a channel, a soul in communion with a silent, sacred world. The "silent congregation of souls" that lived in a portfolio under my bed were born from this meditative state. They were not just drawings; they were the physical evidence of my soul's escape, the artifacts of a deep, focused stillness that saved my life. This was my meditation.

My other sanctuary was my own mind. When the sketchbook wasn't available, I would disappear into visions. This was not just idle daydreaming; it was a profound act of self-preservation, a form of active, visionary meditation. I would build entire worlds behind my eyes where I was safe, loved, and free. I remember sitting on the back of my dad's motorcycle, the world blurring past in a tunnel of trees. I would close my eyes and become a bird, my spirit soaring high above the winding roads, unbound by the fear that so often clung to my small body. The feeling of the wind was not just wind; it was the feeling of flight, of absolute freedom.

I would escape into the intricate, perfect world of the miniature log cabin my father had built. In my mind, I would walk through its tiny rooms, feel the warmth from its cobblestone fireplace, and sleep soundly under its tiny quilts. In that inner world, there were no monsters, no dark hallways, no terrifying silences. There was only the deep, comforting peace of a home my soul so desperately craved. These escapes—into the sky, into a dollhouse, into the hazy blue memory of my granny's mountains—were not a sign of a distracted child. They were the work of a young mystic learning to use her focused consciousness to travel beyond the confines of her painful reality. This, too, was my meditation.

I share this with you because I want you to understand that you have likely been meditating your whole life, too. Where did you go to feel safe? Did you lose yourself for hours in the world of a book? Did you find a strange peace in organizing your toys with meticulous care? Did you walk in the woods, your focus narrowed to the pattern of light filtering through the leaves? Did you dance in your room, your entire being consumed by the music?

These are not frivolous distractions. These are the natural, intuitive ways a soul seeks stillness. These are the gateways to meditation. The goal now is not to learn a new and foreign skill, but to simply bring a conscious awareness to the practice of sanctuary-building that you have already mastered.

So, why is this non-negotiable? Why must we begin our journey into the psychic realm by first building this inner sanctuary of stillness?

Imagine your intuitive system is a highly sensitive, celestial radio. For the person who has experienced trauma, that radio has been left on, full volume, scanning every single frequency at once. The result is a cacophony of static—the fears of your inner child, the anxieties of your present life, the emotional broadcasts of everyone around you, and somewhere, buried deep beneath it all, the clear, quiet signal from the spirit world. It is impossible to discern the true message amidst all that noise.

Meditation is the act of gently turning down the volume on the static. It is the practice of slowly and deliberately tuning your radio dial to a single, clear frequency: the frequency of your own soul.

When you sit in stillness, even for five minutes, you are sending a powerful message to the watchman in your mind. You are telling your amygdala, "Look. We are not running. We are not fighting. We are just sitting here, breathing. And we are safe." With each conscious breath, you are gently retraining a nervous system that has been wired for a war that is now over. You are teaching it the forgotten language of peace. It is only when the watchman finally relaxes his grip on the alarm bell that you can begin to hear the other, more subtle sounds: the gentle whispers of your guides, the intuitive knowing in your gut, the quiet hum of your own spirit.

This practice creates the necessary container for the profound experiences to come. An ungrounded, anxious, and chaotic mind is like a leaky bucket. You can pour the most beautiful spiritual wisdom into it, but it will simply drain away, leaving you feeling more scattered than before. A consistent meditation practice strengthens that container. With each session, you are reinforcing the vessel of your consciousness, making it strong enough to hold the powerful light and information that you are about to invite in.

Before you can confidently navigate the world of spirit, you must first become the unwavering anchor of your own. You must know the feel of your own energy, the sound of your own soul, so that when you connect with another, you do not lose yourself. Meditation is the practice of coming home to yourself, over and over again, until that home becomes an unshakable fortress of peace.

In the chapters that follow, we will explore the architecture of the intuitive brain and learn the practical tools of grounding, shielding, and navigating the four clairs. But all of these tools rest upon this one, foundational practice. Do not see it as a chore, but as an act of profound self-love. See it as a promise you are making to that little girl or boy inside you who never had a safe place to rest.

You are building that safe place now. It is not made of paper or daydreams, but of your own conscious, loving presence. It is a sanctuary within, a quiet room where you can finally take a deep breath and know that you are home. And from the sacred stillness of that room, a whole new universe will begin to speak to you.

CHAPTER FIFTEEN

The Alchemist's Brain:
How Trauma Unlocks Intuition

Throughout my story, you have witnessed how a childhood steeped in fear forced me to develop a heightened awareness—an ability to sense, feel, and know things beyond the ordinary. For years, I simply accepted these skills as part of who I was, a strange and lonely gift born from pain. I didn't have a name for it then, but I now understand that my intuitive abilities were not just a spiritual phenomenon; they were a survival mechanism written into my very biology, forged in the crucible of trauma.

Science is beginning to catch up to what survivors have always known intuitively: that adverse childhood experiences can fundamentally reshape the brain, unlocking extraordinary capacities for perception. It's not magic; it's neuroscience.

At the heart of this transformation is a small, almond-shaped part of our brain called the amygdala. Think of it as the frantic watchman in the watchtower of your mind, the one who sounds the alarm. For a child in a safe and loving home, this alarm sounds only in moments of genuine danger—a fall from a bike, a startling loud noise. The watchman can rest, trusting the quiet. For a child in a constantly unsafe environment, the watchman never rests. The alarm system never shuts off.

For me, that alarm blared every single night. I can still feel the cold dread that would settle in my bones as the house grew quiet, a silence that was never peaceful, only full of waiting. My amygdala was on high alert, scanning my world for the slightest hint of danger. The creak of a floorboard wasn't just the house settling; it was a syllable in a language of threat. The distant smell of stale cigarettes wafting under the door wasn't just a scent; it was a signal that the predator was near. My entire being was an antenna, tuned to a frequency of fear. This state of constant hyper-vigilance is utterly exhausting, but it is also a powerful, if brutal, training ground for the soul.

This wasn't just a nighttime phenomenon. The watchman was on duty during the day, too, constantly at work, reading the unseen. I learned to distinguish between the sounds of safety and the sounds of threat. The clinking of tin pots and laughter from my granny's kitchen in the mountains was the sound of warmth, of biscuits and belonging. The sound of my dad playing his guitar was the sound of connection, a temporary peace. But at home, the sounds were different. The scrape of a chair, the turn of a doorknob, the very quality of the silence—each was data to be analyzed for its potential danger.

Survival required me to become a master at reading the silent, energetic language of my environment. Research has shown that this intense, prolonged stress can lead to structural changes in the brain. The amygdala becomes more sensitive, creating a mind that is exceptionally skilled at detecting non-verbal cues and emotional energy. This is the birthplace of what we call psychic abilities.

Clairsentience:
The Language of Feeling

You learn to feel what others are feeling, to absorb their emotional state as your own. Before I had a word for it, I was clairsentient. I learned to interpret the subtle shift in my sister Lydia's shoulders, to know she was hungry before she ever said a word because I could feel the hollow ache of it myself. I could feel the loneliness radiating from her like a cold draft in a warm room, a quiet sadness that clung to her like a second skin. At Aunt Bee's big purple house, the air was thick with chaotic, joyful energy—loud, messy, and safe. At my own home, the energy was thin and sharp, coiling in the corners of rooms. I learned to feel the sharp edge of Sue's anger long before she ever raised her voice; it was a shift in the atmospheric pressure, a tightening in my own chest that warned me to make myself small, to disappear.

Claircognizance:
The Language of Knowing

You learn to "know" a person's intentions without logical evidence, a gut feeling that screams a warning. This knowing bypasses thought and settles deep in your bones. I learned this language on a long, sun-filled afternoon, dressed in my favorite yellow dress, waiting for my mother. I sat on a kitchen chair by the front door for hours, a hopeful little girl with her teddy bear suitcase. But as the day wore on, another feeling began to bloom beneath the hope—a cold, heavy knowing that settled in my stomach. There was no evidence; no one had called, no car had driven away. But I knew. I knew she wasn't coming long before Sue placed a kind hand on my shoulder and gave the fact a voice. In that moment, the little girl who wanted to believe in promises learned a harder, more reliable truth: to trust the feeling that arrives without reason, because that feeling is the unvarnished truth.

Clairaudience:
The Language of Hearing the Unspoken

You learn to hear the unspoken, the intent behind the silence, the threat in a seemingly normal footstep. After one of Sue's beatings, I heard my dad's weak voice from the doorway: "You need to listen to your mother so this doesn't happen again." The words themselves were a simple command. But what I heard clairaudiently was a symphony of his abdication: his fear, his weakness, his inability to protect me. I heard the surrender in his tone, the plea for me to just comply so he wouldn't have to confront the monster in our home. Years later, Lydia would give this gift a name. When I told her about my angel portraits, she said, "You weren't just quiet, Kathy. You were listening. To everything. The things people weren't even saying." She had seen the watchman in the tower, listening not just with her ears, but with her entire being.

Clairvoyance:
The Language of Seeing Beyond

And sometimes, when the threat is imminent, your mind learns to see beyond the confines of your own body. To survive those nights, I remember ascending from my body, disconnected from the action, floating near the ceiling where I could not be touched. It was a desperate act of self-preservation, the genesis of clairvoyance—an ability born not from a desire to see the future, but from a desperate need to survive the present. This skill, forged in trauma, later evolved.

It allowed me to see Grandma McCade's spirit, healthy and whole, sitting on my bed after she passed. It allowed me to see the single, silent star twinkle into existence in my office, a thank you from a baby angel whose portrait I had drawn. The out-of-body experience of a terrified child became the spirit-sight of a healing woman.

These are not superpowers you are born with; they are skills forged in the fire when the world around you is a minefield of unpredictable adults.

Of course, this brilliant adaptation has its echoes, its ghosts that follow you into the safety of adulthood. A brain wired to expect danger will find it, even when it isn't there. My husband loves to tell the story of one of our first nights together. I was asleep when he simply lifted his head to peer over my shoulder. He didn't touch me, but the moment his gaze fell upon me, my eyes shot open and I let out a deep, guttural gasp of sheer terror. He was so frightened he bolted out of bed. We laugh about it now—his "Exorcist moment"—but it's a perfect example of an amygdala that has been trained for decades to interpret any unexpected presence in the dark as a life-or-death threat. The watchman in my mind was still on duty, loyal to a war that had ended long ago.

Understanding this science has been a profound part of my own healing. For so long, I believed my hyper-sensitivity was a flaw, that I was somehow broken or too fragile for this world. The little girl who made herself invisible came to believe she deserved to be unseen. The knowledge that my brain had not broken, but had instead brilliantly adapted to protect me, was liberating. My psychic abilities were not a random quirk; they were a testament to the resilience of a little girl who learned to see in the dark because she had no other choice.

Now that you understand the science and the story behind this sacred alchemy, our journey shifts from understanding to practice. Over the next few chapters, I will give you the practical tools, exercises, and experiments I have developed over a lifetime of listening in the dark. Together, we will learn to tune the sensitive instrument of your nervous system, transforming the echoes of your trauma response into a clear channel for psychic power. The watchman in your mind will not be dismissed, but retrained—from a sentinel of fear to a seer of truth. It is time to reclaim the power that has been inside you all along.

Come with me. I'll leave the light on for you.

References
- Cleveland Clinic. (2023). Amygdala. https://my.clevelandclinic.org/health/body/24894-amygdala
- Bremner, J. D. (2006). Traumatic stress: effects on the brain. Dialogues in Clinical Neuroscience, 8(4), 445–461. https://pmc.ncbi.nlm.nih.gov/articles/PMC6131660/
- Teicher, M. H., Samson, J. A., Anderson, C. M., & Ohashi, K. (2016). The effects of childhood maltreatment on brain structure, function and connectivity. Nature Reviews Neuroscience, 17(10), 652–666. https://pubmed.ncbi.nlm.nih.gov/22112927/
- Van der Kolk, B. A. (2003). The neurobiology of childhood trauma and abuse. Child and Adolescent Psychiatric Clinics of North America, 12(2), 293–317. https://pubmed.ncbi.nlm.nih.gov/18982530/

CHAPTER SIXTEEN

Building Your Sanctuary:
Psychic Protection and Grounding

Throughout my story, you have witnessed how a child in a constant state of fear becomes an antenna. I absorbed the silent, suffocating anxiety in a room, felt the impending rage before a hand was ever raised, and learned to navigate the emotional minefield of my home by becoming a master of reading the unseen. My nervous system became a seismograph, registering the slightest tremors of danger in my environment.

For those of us who grew up this way, opening up to the spirit world can feel terrifying. Why would we willingly make our antenna even more sensitive? Why would we open the door to more unseen energies when we've spent a lifetime trying to protect ourselves from them?

This is why the very first step in any psychic development is not about opening up, but about learning how to feel safe. It is the most important, non-negotiable step in this entire journey. For years, my abilities were a raw, reactive survival mechanism. It was only when I learned to create a sanctuary within myself that they transformed into a conscious, sacred gift. This chapter is about giving you the tools to build your own sanctuary. This isn't about building walls out of fear; it's about creating a safe and sacred container, out of love, for the beautiful soul that you are. Before we can learn to hear the whispers of spirit, we must first learn to quiet the noise of fear.

Grounding:
The Sacred Anchor

One of the primary ways I survived my childhood was by leaving my body. When the reality of a moment was too painful to endure, my spirit would float away. I would disappear into the flight of a starling, into the quiet world of my sketchbook, anywhere but here. This disassociation is a brilliant and necessary coping mechanism, but in adulthood, it can leave us feeling untethered, anxious, and disconnected from our own lives.

The antidote to this feeling is grounding. Grounding is the conscious act of anchoring your spirit back into your physical body and connecting your energy to the stable, loving energy of the Earth. It is a declaration to the universe and to yourself: "I am here. I am present. I am safe in this body, right now."

I didn't have a name for it then, but my most profound moments of peace as a child were moments of grounding. I remember the feel of the cool, damp earth beneath my bare feet at my granny's farm, the blades of grass tickling my toes. It was a physical connection to something solid and real when everything else in my life felt chaotic and uncertain. In those moments, I felt like one of the trees on her property, my own invisible roots sinking deep into the soil, drawing strength and stability from the ground beneath me. That is the feeling we are going to cultivate now.

EXERCISE 1: THE ROOT CORD VISUALIZATION

This is a simple yet powerful exercise you can do anytime you feel anxious, overwhelmed, or energetically scattered.

1. **Find a quiet space.** You can sit in a chair with your feet flat on the floor or stand with your knees slightly bent. If you can do this outside with your bare feet on the grass or soil, the effect will be even more profound.
2. **Close your eyes and breathe.** Take three slow, deep breaths. With each inhale, imagine you are breathing in peace. With each exhale, imagine you are releasing tension and fear. Settle into the stillness of your own body.
3. **Visualize the cord.** Bring your awareness to the base of your spine. From this point, imagine a thick cord of light—like the trunk of an ancient tree—growing downwards, out of your body. See it moving easily through the floor, through the foundation of your building, and deep into the earth below.
4. **Anchor yourself.** Watch as this cord of light travels deeper and deeper, past the topsoil, past the rock, down into the very heart of the Earth. Imagine it wrapping itself securely around the Earth's molten, crystalline core. Feel the anchor take hold. You are now securely connected.
5. **Release and Receive.** Through this cord, allow any heavy, anxious, or foreign energy within you to flow down and away, to be safely recycled by the Earth. On your next inhale, imagine drawing the Earth's calm, stable, and nurturing energy up through your cord, into your body. Feel it fill your feet, your legs, and your entire being with a sense of solid, unshakable peace.
6. **Return.** When you feel calm and centered, gently thank the Earth. You can leave the cord connected for as long as you like,

knowing you are anchored and supported. When you are ready, slowly open your eyes.

Psychic Shielding:
The Sanctuary Within

As a child, I built sanctuaries out of whatever I could find—a sketchbook, a pile of pillows, the imaginary world of my Barbie doll. These were my safe spaces. Psychic shielding is the act of creating that same kind of sanctuary, but on an energetic level. It is a conscious bubble of protection that you create around yourself to keep your own energy field clear and sovereign.

This is not about living in fear or paranoia. Think of it like washing your hands. You do it to maintain your physical hygiene. Shielding is about maintaining your energetic hygiene. It's especially important for those of us who are naturally empathetic and tend to absorb the emotional states of others. A shield allows you to move through the world, even through crowded or chaotic environments, without taking on everyone else's "stuff."

EXERCISE 2: THE BUBBLE OF LIGHT

This visualization is best done at the beginning of your day, but you can use it anytime you know you're about to enter a stressful situation.

1. **Ground yourself.** Begin with a few deep breaths or a quick version of the Root Cord exercise. It's always best to shield from a grounded state.
2. **Call in the light.** Imagine a brilliant, beautiful star of light descending from the heavens, shining down directly above your

head. Choose a color that feels loving and protective to you—shimmering gold, brilliant white, or a soft pink.

3. **Form the bubble.** Allow this light to flow down and all around you, forming a beautiful, resilient bubble or egg-shaped sphere that completely surrounds your body, extending about an arm's length in every direction. See it shimmer and glow with protective energy.

4. **Set the intention.** This is the most important step. As you visualize this bubble, set a clear intention for it. You can say silently in your mind: "This shield of light protects me from all negative and foreign energies. Only energies of love and for my highest good may enter. I am safe. I am sovereign. I am protected."

5. **Reinforce and go.** Feel the truth of those words. Know that you are safe within your sanctuary. Now, go about your day. At the end of the day, you can visualize a gentle rain of light washing your bubble clean of anything it may have picked up.

Managing Empathy:
Distinguishing Your Energy from Theirs

For those of us who grew up in volatile environments, empathy was not a choice; it was a survival tool. We became energetic sponges, soaking up the moods and intentions of those around us to predict their behavior and keep ourselves safe. The problem is, as adults, we often forget to "wring out the sponge." We walk around carrying the weight of everyone else's anger, sadness, and anxiety, and we mistake it for our own.

Learning to manage this profound empathy is the key to transforming it from a draining liability into a powerful psychic gift. The first step is simply learning to ask the question: "Is this mine?"

EXERCISE 3: THE ENERGETIC INVENTORY

This is a practice of mindful self-awareness that you can do multiple times a day, especially after interacting with others or being in a public place.

1. **Pause and breathe.** Take a moment to stop what you are doing. Close your eyes if you can and take one deep, cleansing breath.
2. **Scan your body.** Bring your awareness inside your body. How do you feel? Is there a tightness in your chest? A pit in your stomach? A heaviness in your shoulders?
3. **Ask the question.** Ask yourself, with genuine curiosity: "Is this feeling mine?" You might be surprised by the immediate answer that pops into your head. Often, the first intuitive hit is the correct one.
4. **Get specific.** If you suspect the feeling isn't yours, ask a follow-up question: "Whose energy does this feel like?" You might get an image of a coworker you just spoke with, or a family member you were thinking about.
5. **Release with gratitude.** If you determine you've picked up someone else's energy, you don't need to judge it. Simply acknowledge it. You can say, "I recognize that this is not my energy to carry. I release it now with love and send it back to its source, cleansed and healed."

EXERCISE 4: THE CORD-CUTTING VISUALIZATION

We are all connected to others through energetic cords. Healthy cords are conduits for love and support. Unhealthy or draining cords can leave us feeling depleted. This exercise is a powerful way to reclaim your energy.

1. **Get comfortable.** Find a quiet space and ground yourself.
2. **Visualize the cords.** Imagine your own body of light. Now, see if you can perceive any energetic cords extending from you to other people, places, or situations. Don't worry if you can't see them clearly; just intend to become aware of them. You might sense them as threads, ropes, or tubes of energy.
3. **Call in your tool.** Imagine in your hand a tool for loving detachment. This could be a pair of golden scissors, a sword made of pure white light, or even the hand of an angel.
4. **Cut with love.** One by one, gently and lovingly, use your tool to cut each cord that feels draining or unhealthy. As you cut each one, you can say, "I release what is no longer mine. I reclaim my energy now. I send you back your energy, and I take back mine." See the ends of the cords on your body heal over with beautiful, golden light.
5. **Fill with your own light.** Once you are free, imagine your entire being filling up with your own radiant, pure energy. Feel yourself whole and complete within your own sanctuary.

These practices—grounding, shielding, and managing your empathy—are not one-time fixes. They are a new way of life. Each time you ground yourself, you are telling that little girl or boy inside that they are safe now. Each time you shield, you are honoring your own sacred space. And each time you release energy that is not yours, you are lovingly re-parenting yourself. You are building the safe house you never had. And from within its sacred walls, you will finally be able to hear the loving whispers of the universe.

CHAPTER SEVENTEEN

The Four Clairs:
Learning the Language of Spirit

In the silent, watchful world of my childhood, I had to learn a language that was not spoken with words. It was a language of feeling, of seeing what wasn't there, of hearing the whispers beneath the silence, and of knowing things without knowing how I knew. This was not a gift I was taught; it was a dialect I mastered out of necessity, a secret tongue I shared with survival.

Today, I understand that this is the native language of the soul. It is a language we all possess, though for many, it has been muted by the noise of the outside world or suppressed by the logic of the conscious mind. This language is communicated through four primary channels, often called the "four clairs."

Think of them not as strange, mystical powers, but as the intuitive senses of your spirit. Just as you have five physical senses to navigate the material world, you have these intuitive senses to navigate the world of energy and spirit. For those of us who have experienced trauma, these senses were often forced into a state of high alert. They became our radar, our early warning system. Now, in the safety of our sanctuary, we can learn to work with them consciously, to transform them from a reactive alarm system into a beautiful and reliable inner compass.

In this chapter, we will gently explore each of these four senses. You will likely find that one or two feel more natural to you than the others. That is perfectly normal. We all have a dominant intuitive sense, just as some of us are more visual or more auditory in our daily lives. The goal is not to become a master of all four overnight, but to simply begin to recognize the sound of your own soul speaking.

Clairsentience:
The Language of Feeling

Clairsentience, or "clear feeling," is the most common of all intuitive abilities. It is the ability to feel the emotional states of other people, places, or even spirits as if they were your own. It is the language of the energetic sponge.

This was my primary language as a child. Before I could understand the complex dynamics of the adults around me, I could feel them. I remember the oppressive weight of unspoken sadness in our house, a heaviness that seemed to cling to the furniture. I could feel the sharp, coiled energy of Sue's anger radiating from her long before she ever spoke a word. It was a physical sensation, a knot in my stomach that told me to make myself small, to disappear. This profound empathy was my greatest survival tool.

The challenge of clairsentience is learning to distinguish what is yours from what is not. In the last chapter, we practiced releasing energy. Now, we will practice consciously tuning into this sense in a safe and controlled way, transforming it from an unconscious burden into a conscious gift.

EXERCISE 1: THE ENERGY OF A ROOM

This is a simple practice to begin consciously flexing your clairsentient muscle.

1. **Pause at the threshold.** The next time you are about to walk into a room—be it a coffee shop, your office, or a room in your own home—take a moment to pause before you enter.
2. **Ground and tune in.** Close your eyes for just a second. Take a deep breath and connect to your own energy. Now, with the intention of sensing, extend your awareness into the room beyond the door.
3. **Feel the atmosphere.** Without judging or analyzing, simply notice what you feel. Does the energy feel light, heavy, calm, chaotic, happy, or tense? Is it buzzing with activity or still and quiet? There is no right or wrong answer. Just notice the texture of the energy.
4. **Enter and observe.** Now, open your eyes and walk into the room. See how your initial feeling compares to the reality of what is happening. This practice, over time, will build your confidence in your ability to accurately read the energy of a space.

EXERCISE 2: THE STORY OF AN OBJECT (PSYCHOMETRY)

Every object, especially one that has been held or loved, carries an energetic imprint of its owner. This exercise helps you learn to read that energy.

1. **Choose an object.** Select a piece of jewelry, a photograph, or another small object that belongs to a friend or family member (with their permission). It's best to choose something that has

been with them for a long time.

2. **Find your quiet space.** Sit comfortably, ground yourself, and hold the object in your hands.

3. **Set your intention.** Close your eyes. Take a few deep breaths and set the intention to connect with the story and the energy of this object.

4. **Feel and receive.** As you hold the object, simply be open to whatever feelings, emotions, or even images come to you. You might feel a wave of happiness, a pang of sadness, or see a flash of a memory associated with the object. Don't force it. Just allow.

5. **Share and validate.** When you are done, share what you felt with the object's owner. You may be surprised at how your feelings align with the object's true history.

Clairvoyance:
The Language of Seeing

Clairvoyance, or "clear seeing," is the ability to see with the mind's eye. This isn't usually like watching a high-definition movie. More often, it's like a fleeting image in a daydream, a symbol that flashes in your mind, or a memory that doesn't belong to you.

My first conscious clairvoyant experience was seeing my Grandma McCade standing in my doorway after she had passed. It was not a dream. The quality of the image was different—more solid, more real, imbued with a feeling of peace that was unmistakable. My art has always been my most powerful clairvoyant tool. Often, when drawing the Angel Portraits, I would "see" the face in my mind before my pencil ever touched the paper. The image would appear, fully formed, waiting to be brought into the physical world. It was a vision from my soul's sketchbook.

EXERCISE 1: THE MEMORY MOVIE

This is a safe and gentle way to begin activating your third eye, the energetic center of clairvoyance located between your eyebrows.

1. **Choose a happy memory.** Think of a joyful, vivid memory from your life—a birthday party, a day at the beach, a hug from a loved one.
2. **Close your eyes and watch.** Get comfortable and allow yourself to replay this memory in your mind as if it were a movie.
3. **Focus on the details.** Don't just remember what happened; see it. What colors were you wearing? What did the light look like? Can you see the expressions on people's faces? The more you practice recalling visual details from your own past, the stronger your inner sight will become for seeing things from the spirit world.

EXERCISE 2: THE CLOUD GAME

This is a playful way to encourage your brain to find meaningful images in random patterns.

1. **Find your canvas.** Lie on your back and look at the clouds, or simply gaze at a textured surface like a wooden door, a stucco ceiling, or the patterns in a marble countertop.
2. **Soften your gaze.** Don't try to find anything. Simply relax your eyes and let your mind wander.
3. **Allow images to emerge.** Be open to what you see. You might see faces, animals, symbols, or objects. The first image that pops into your head is often a gentle nudge from your intuition. This practice helps you learn to trust the spontaneous images that come from your spirit

Clairaudience:
The Language of Hearing

Clairaudience, or "clear hearing," is the ability to hear messages from the spirit world. This is perhaps the most misunderstood of the clairs. It is very rarely a booming, external voice. Most often, it is a subtle, internal whisper. It can sound like your own thought, but the quality is different—it's often calmer, more concise, and more loving than your own mental chatter. It can also come as a song that gets stuck in your head, or a name that you hear over and over.

My most direct experiences with clairaudience came during the creation of the Angel Portraits. I remember so clearly the little boy who gave me specific, detailed instructions on how to draw his hair and wings. His voice was not in my ears; it was in my mind, a clear, gentle, and persistent thought that was distinctly not my own.

EXERCISE 1: LISTENING TO THE LAYERS OF SILENCE

This is a meditation to help you distinguish between the different sounds within your own mind.

1. **Sit in silence.** Find a quiet place and sit for five minutes.
2. **Listen externally.** For the first minute, just listen to the sounds around you—the hum of the refrigerator, a distant car, the birds outside.
3. **Listen internally.** Now, turn your attention inward. Listen to the frantic, busy thoughts of your own mind—your to-do list, your worries, your plans for dinner. This is your "monkey mind."
4. **Listen deeper.** For the last few minutes, ask your spirit guides or your higher self to make their presence known. Now, listen for

the sounds beneath the chatter. You might "hear" a single word, a feeling of peace, or a gentle sense of love. The goal is to learn to recognize the calm, quiet whisper that is different from the loud noise of your ego.

EXERCISE 2: ASK AND RECEIVE

1. **Ask a simple question.** Before you go to sleep at night, ask your guides a simple, non-emotional question. For example, "What is one thing I need to know for tomorrow?"
2. **Let it go.** Don't try to answer it. Simply release the question to the universe.
3. **Listen upon waking.** When you first wake up, before your mind gets busy, pay attention to the very first thought, song, or word that comes into your head. This is often the answer, delivered to you in the quiet space between sleep and waking.

Claircognizance:
The Language of Knowing

Claircognizance, or "clear knowing," is the ability to know something with absolute certainty, without any logical explanation or proof. It is a divine download of information, an unshakable truth that simply arrives in your consciousness, fully formed.

This was the clair that kept me alive. It was the "cold, heavy knowing" that settled in my stomach as I waited for my mother, a certainty that she was not coming long before Sue ever confirmed it. It was the gut feeling that told me not to trust someone, even when they were smiling. It was an inner compass forged in an environment where my survival depended on knowing the truth, even when everyone around me was lying.

EXERCISE 1: THE FIRST-INSTINCT GAME

This is a playful way to practice trusting that initial hit of information before your logical mind has a chance to doubt it.

1. When the phone rings, before you look at it, ask yourself, "Who is this?"
2. When you're trying to decide what to eat, ask, "What does my body truly need right now?"
3. When you can't find your keys, close your eyes and ask, "Where are they?" and go to the very first place that pops into your head.

The point of this game is not to be right 100% of the time. The point is to get into the habit of paying attention to and honoring that first, instantaneous flash of knowing.

EXERCISE 2: INTUITIVE JOURNALING

1. **Pose a question.** Open a notebook and write a question at the top of the page. It could be something like, "What is the next step on my healing journey?" or "What message does my soul have for me today?"
2. **Set a timer.** Set a timer for five or ten minutes.
3. **Write without stopping.** For the entire duration of the timer, write down everything that comes into your head. Do not pause, do not edit, and do not judge. Even if you have to write "I don't know what to write" over and over, keep the pen moving. This practice helps to bypass the conscious, analytical mind and allows the deeper wisdom of your claircognizance to flow onto the page.

Remember, these are not four separate powers. They are four

interconnected streams that flow from the same source: your soul. As you begin to practice these exercises, be gentle with yourself. You are not just learning a new skill; you are reawakening a sacred, ancient part of yourself. You are learning to trust the language you were born speaking.

CHAPTER EIGHTEEN

Opening the Channel:
An Introduction to Mediumship

The most profound discovery of my journey was not that I could see or hear spirits; it was that the conversation never truly ends. When I first began drawing the Angel Portraits, I thought I was simply creating art, offering a small comfort to the grieving. But as I sat with my pencils, a quiet and holy space would open up. I soon realized I was not alone in my studio. I was a guest, a witness, a scribe. I was not just drawing a memory of a child; I was in a living, breathing conversation with their soul.

This is the heart of mediumship. It is not about "contacting the dead." It is about recognizing that love, like energy, cannot be destroyed. It simply changes form. Mediumship is the sacred act of becoming a bridge between those forms, a conduit for the love that continues to flow, a telephone line to heaven.

For many, this is the most intimidating step on the intuitive path. The idea of intentionally connecting with the spirit world can bring up deep-seated fears, images from horror movies, or a sense of stepping into a realm where we do not belong. I understand that fear. For years, the unseen was a source of terror for me. But I have come to know, with every fiber of my being, that the spirit world you connect with through love is a place of profound peace, intelligence, and unconditional acceptance.

In this chapter, we are not going to fling the door to the spirit world wide open. We are simply going to learn how to knock, gently and lovingly, and how to listen for the answer. This is not a performance; it is a prayer. It is an act of service, and it must always, always begin with a sacred intention.

Setting the Intention:
The Sacred Welcome Mat

Before you invite any guest into your home, you make sure the space is clean, welcoming, and safe. Connecting with the spirit world is no different. Setting a clear and loving intention is the most important part of mediumship. It is your welcome mat, your bouncer, and your declaration of purpose all in one. It establishes the rules of engagement and ensures that you are only connecting with energies that are for your highest and best good.

When I begin a portrait, I never just start drawing. I first create a sacred space. Sometimes it's as simple as lighting a candle and saying a quiet prayer. Other times, it's a more involved ritual of calling in my own spirit guides and the angels. This act of preparation is a signal to the universe. It says, "I am opening this channel for the purpose of healing and love. Only beings of the highest light and vibration are welcome here."

This is not a step to be rushed or skipped. Your intention is your energetic shield and your homing beacon. It filters out any lower vibrational energies and attracts the loving souls you wish to connect with.

EXERCISE 1: THE INVITATION OF LIGHT

Use this exercise anytime you wish to open a gentle channel for communication. This is your ritual for putting out the sacred welcome mat.

1. **Prepare Your Space.** Find a quiet place where you will not be disturbed. You may wish to light a candle, play soft instrumental music, or hold a favorite crystal. Do whatever makes you feel safe, peaceful, and centered.
2. **Ground and Protect.** Begin by grounding yourself with the Root Cord visualization from Chapter 16. Then, create your Bubble of Light around you. You are now in a clean, protected, and sovereign energetic space.
3. **Call in Your Team.** Close your eyes and speak from your heart. You can say these words aloud or in your mind: "I call upon my highest, most loving spirit guides, guardian angels, and any ancestors who are working for my greatest good. Please surround me now in a circle of pure, divine, white light. Protect me, guide me, and help me to be a clear and loving channel for healing." Take a moment to feel their presence. You might feel a sense of warmth, a tingling sensation, or just a deep feeling of peace. Know that you are not alone.
4. **Set the Specific Intention.** Now, state clearly who you wish to connect with and why. For example: "I now open this channel with love and invite the spirit of my grandmother, [Her Name], to step forward if she is willing and it is for the highest good of all. I wish to feel her love and receive any message of comfort she may have for me."

5. **Hold the Space.** Your space is now set. You have created a beautiful, high-vibrational temple for communication. You are ready to listen.

Receiving and Interpreting Messages:
The Art of Listening

Once you have set your sacred intention, the next step is to simply be still and listen. This is often the most challenging part, as our busy, analytical minds want to jump in and ask, "Am I just making this up?" This is a normal and valid question. Learning to differentiate the subtle voice of spirit from the loud voice of your own mind is the art of mediumship.

From my experience drawing the portraits, I've learned that spirit communication has a different "flavor" than my own thoughts.

It is gentle and persistent. My own thoughts can be frantic and scattered. A message from spirit is often a calm, repetitive whisper. The little boy who was so insistent about his hair didn't shout; he just gently and persistently repeated his request until I got it right.

It is often simple and loving. The ego-mind can be complex, critical, and story-driven. Spirit messages are usually concise, simple, and always, always rooted in love. They are meant to comfort, not to confuse or frighten.

It comes in through your dominant clair. As we learned in the last chapter, spirit will speak to you in the language you understand best. If you are clairsentient, you will likely feel their presence and their emotions. If you are clairvoyant, you may see a fleeting image of them in your mind's eye. Pay attention to how the information arrives.

EXERCISE 2: THE MEMORY BOX

This is a safe and beautiful way to practice connecting with a specific loved one in spirit. It is an exercise in receiving, not forcing.

1. **Create your sacred space.** Use the "Invitation of Light" exercise to set your intention to connect with one specific person in spirit whom you loved and trusted in life.

2. **Hold a memory.** Bring to mind a favorite, joyful memory of this person. Don't just think about it; feel it. Feel the love you have for them. See their smile in your mind's eye. This feeling of love is the frequency that they will recognize and be drawn to.

3. **Make a gentle request.** In your mind, ask them for a sign of their presence. You could say, "If you are here with me now, could you please give me a sign? Could you let me feel your love, or share a memory with me that will let me know it's you?"

4. **Be a receptive satellite dish.** Now, let go. Do not strain or search for an answer. Simply sit in a state of open, loving awareness for five to ten minutes. Pay attention to any subtle shifts.

Do you suddenly feel a wave of peace or a specific emotion you associate with them? (Clairsentience)

Does a forgotten memory of them pop into your head? (Clairvoyance)

Does a song they loved start playing in your mind? (Clairaudience)

Do you just get a sudden, unshakable knowing that they are with you? (Claircognizance)

Give thanks and release. When you are done, thank your loved one for their presence. Release the connection by grounding yourself again, perhaps by placing your hands on your knees and feeling your feet on the floor. Thank your spirit team and close the circle of light.

Creative Channeling:
Your Soul's Signature

For me, the pencil is a lightning rod. My sketchbook is a portal. Art has always been my most natural and powerful form of mediumship. When I am drawing a portrait, my conscious, analytical mind is so focused on the technical aspects—the shading, the proportions, the texture—that it gets out of the way, allowing my soul and the spirit I am connecting with to flow through my hand and onto the page.

You, too, have a unique channel. Your soul has a signature way of expressing itself. You do not need to be a professional artist or writer to use creativity as a tool for spirit communication. The act of creating quiets the ego and allows the intuitive mind to come forward.

EXERCISE 3: THE UNSENT LETTER (AUTOMATIC WRITING)

This is a powerful and gentle form of channeled writing.

1. **Set your sacred space.** Use the "Invitation of Light" exercise to invite a specific loved one in spirit to communicate with you.
2. **Prepare your tools.** Open a notebook to a blank page or sit in front of a blank computer screen. At the top of the page, write a greeting, such as, "Dear Mom," or "Dearest [Name]."
3. **Begin the conversation.** Start by writing a letter to them from your heart. Tell them what you're feeling, how much you miss

them, what's been happening in your life. Pour your love onto the page.

4. **Invite a response.** After you have written for a while, write a question. For example, "What message do you have for me today?" or "Is there anything you want me to know?"

5. **Let your hand move.** Now, take a deep breath and surrender. Allow your hand to write whatever comes. Do not judge it, do not edit it, and do not stop to think about it. Let the words flow, even if they don't make sense at first. You are simply taking dictation from your soul and their spirit. Keep writing until you feel the energy complete.

6. **Read with your heart.** When you are finished, read back what you have written. Often, you will find a wisdom, a turn of phrase, or a loving message that feels distinctly different from your own conscious thoughts.

Remember, mediumship is a practice, not a perfection. It is a relationship with the spirit world that you cultivate over time, built on a foundation of trust, love, and reverence. Be patient and compassionate with yourself. Just as I spent years with my "silent congregation of souls" under my bed, you may spend time simply sitting in the quiet, feeling their presence, long before any clear messages come through. That is okay. In fact, that is beautiful. You are simply remembering how to listen to the eternal, unending conversation of love.

CHAPTER NINETEEN

Beyond the Veil:
Exploring Out-of-Body Awareness

I learned to leave my body the way a fledgling bird learns to leave the nest—out of a terrifying, primal necessity. When the footsteps grew closer and the stale scent of cigarettes slipped under my door, the four walls of my bedroom became a cage. My small, seven-year-old body was a trap. To survive the unbearable, my spirit learned to unmoor itself.

I would disappear.

I'd feel a strange, humming vibration, a loosening, and then I would be free. I would become that quicksilver starling, my consciousness darting and dipping through the crystal blue sky of my inner world. In those moments, I was not a terrified little girl in a dark room; I was pure awareness, boundless and untouched. This was not a conscious choice. It was a reflex of a soul that refused to be broken. I was not practicing a spiritual technique; I was enacting a survival strategy of the highest order.

This profound ability to disconnect, known clinically as

disassociation, is a brilliant adaptation of a mind under siege. But what if this desperate act of escape is simply the untrained, reactive version of a profound and natural human ability? What if the very mechanism that allowed you to survive your past could be consciously and intentionally transformed into a sacred tool for exploring the vastness of your own soul and the universe itself?

This is the alchemy of out-of-body awareness. It is the act of reclaiming the flight reflex and turning it into a conscious, soul-led journey. This chapter is an invitation to explore that possibility, gently and safely. We will not be running from anything. We will be learning to consciously step beyond the veil, with intention and love, to discover that we are so much more than our physical bodies.

Understanding the Landscape:
Dreams, Imagination, and OBEs

Before we begin, it's important to understand the landscape of inner experience. Our minds are vast, and it's easy to get lost without a map. Let's distinguish between three common states of non-physical awareness.

Dreaming: When you are dreaming, you are largely a passive observer. The subconscious mind is the director, projecting a film onto the screen of your awareness. The narratives are often illogical, symbolic, and you typically don't realize you are dreaming until you wake up.

Imagination/Visualization: This is an active, conscious process. When you visualize, you are the director. You are creating the images, crafting the story, and guiding the experience with your conscious mind. It is a powerful tool for creation and manifestation.

Out-of-Body Experience (OBE) / Astral Projection: This is a state of conscious observation. You are fully aware that your center of consciousness is separate from your physical body. You are not creating the environment; you are perceiving it from a different vantage point. The experience feels profoundly real, often more real than waking life, and you have a sense of agency and independent thought.

My childhood experiences were a raw form of OBE, triggered by trauma. Now, we will learn to approach this state not with fear, but with curiosity and a sacred intention.

The Alchemist's Compass:
Safety, Intention, and the Silver Cord

I cannot stress this enough: you do not ever have to do this. Your sanctuary is your own, and you are always in control. If exploring out-of-body awareness does not feel right for you, then honor that. For those who feel a gentle curiosity, the following practices are your compass, ensuring that your explorations are always safe, protected, and for your highest good.

The number one rule is that we never attempt this from a place of fear or a desire to escape our lives. We do this from a place of wholeness, curiosity, and a desire for spiritual expansion. This is why the grounding and shielding work from Chapter 16 is an absolute prerequisite.

The Silver Cord: In all traditions that teach out-of-body travel, there is the concept of the "silver cord." It is a luminous, infinitely elastic thread of light that connects your energy body to your physical body.

It is your tether, your lifeline. It can never be broken, and it will always guide you safely back. Simply knowing it is there can be a profound comfort. Before any practice, you can set the intention to become aware of this beautiful, shimmering cord connecting your spirit to your form.

EXERCISE 1: THE CIRCLE OF SAFE PASSAGE

This is an essential ritual to perform before any intentional out-of-body exploration. It expands on our previous protection exercises to create a specific container for this sacred work.

1. **Prepare Your Physical Space.** Choose a time and place where you will be completely undisturbed for at least 30 minutes. Your bed or a comfortable recliner is ideal. Unplug your phone. Ensure the room is a comfortable temperature.

2. **Ground and Shield.** Perform the Root Cord and Bubble of Light exercises. Create your baseline of safety.

3. **Call in Your Travel Guides.** Just as you have a spirit team for mediumship, you have guides who specialize in interdimensional travel. Expand your invitation: "I call upon my highest, most loving spirit guides, guardian angels, and any beings of light who are masters of safe spiritual travel. I ask you to create a sacred and impenetrable circle of protection around my physical body and my energy body as I undertake this journey. Please ensure that my exploration is for my highest good, and guide me safely back when my work is complete."

4. **Set Your Intention.** Be very clear about your goal. A simple, gentle intention is best for beginners. For example: "My intention is to gently and lovingly separate my consciousness from my physical body, to float to the ceiling of this room to observe, and to return safely and with full memory of the experience."

5. **State Your Sovereignty.** End with a declaration of your power. "I am a sovereign being of light. I am in complete control of this experience. I will only connect with energies of the highest love, and I can return to my body instantly at any time by simply willing it."

6. **Your space is now prepared.** You have created a sacred temple for your soul's journey.

First Steps Beyond the Body:
The Floating Leaf

The key to a conscious OBE is profound physical relaxation and a focused, yet gentle, state of mind. The goal is not to "try" to leave your body; that kind of effort creates tension. The goal is to relax so deeply that your spirit body can naturally float free.

EXERCISE 2: THE FLOATING LEAF

1. **Create Your Circle of Safe Passage.** Do not skip this step.
2. **Relax Your Body.** Lie down comfortably on your back. Starting with your toes and working your way up to your head, consciously tense and then release each muscle group. Tense your feet for a count of five, then release completely. Tense your calves, then release. Continue this all the way up to your jaw and scalp until your entire body feels heavy and deeply relaxed.
3. **Focus on Your Breath.** Bring your awareness to your breath. Don't change it; just observe it. Feel the gentle rise and fall of your chest. With each exhale, allow yourself to sink deeper and deeper into a state of peace.
4. **Enter the Vibrational State.** As you drift into the state between waking and sleeping (the hypnagogic state), you may begin to

feel a subtle humming or vibration in your body. This is a very common sign that your energy body is beginning to separate from your physical body. Do not be alarmed. If you feel it, simply observe it with curiosity. Welcome it as a sign that you are on the right track.

5. **Visualize the Leaf.** Now, begin a gentle visualization. Imagine your consciousness is as light as a single, dry leaf. Feel the "lightness" of your awareness.

6. **Invite the Float.** Gently, without straining, invite this leafy lightness to float upwards. Imagine a soft breeze lifting you. Your intention is not to go far, just to float up a few feet, towards the ceiling.

7. **Observe.** If you achieve separation, your first goal is simply to observe. Turn your awareness around and look down at your physical body resting peacefully below. Notice the details of the room from this new perspective. The goal is to remain calm and curious.

8. **Return with a Thought.** When you are ready to return, all you need to do is think about your physical body, specifically your fingers or toes. Your consciousness will snap back into place instantly and gently.

9. **Record Your Experience.** Lie still for a few moments, integrating the experience. Then, immediately write down everything you can remember in a journal.

Be patient with this process. It may take many attempts to achieve a conscious separation. The goal is the practice itself—the deep relaxation and the focused intention.

Remote Viewing:
Seeing with the Soul's Eyes

As a child, to know what was happening in the other room, I would send my awareness out ahead of me. I could "see" and "feel" the emotional landscape of the house without ever leaving my bed. This is the essence of remote viewing—the ability to perceive a person, place, or object at a distance using your intuitive senses. It is a focused application of out-of-body awareness.

EXERCISE 3: THE PARTNERED POSTCARD

This is a wonderful beginner's exercise that provides you with clear feedback. You will need a trusted friend to be your partner.

1. **The Sender's Role.** Have your friend (the sender) choose a postcard or a photograph with a simple, clear image (e.g., a beach, a mountain, a cityscape). At a pre-arranged time, they should sit quietly with the image for 5-10 minutes, looking at it and intending to "send" the visual and emotional information to you.

2. **The Receiver's Role.** At the same time, in your own quiet space, perform your "Circle of Safe Passage" ritual. Set the clear intention: "My intention is to safely and lovingly connect with the information my friend [Friend's Name] is sending me now."

3. **Receive Impressions.** Sit with a notebook and pen. Relax and allow impressions to come to you. Do not try to guess the image. Instead, pay attention to the raw data your clairs provide:

4. **Clairsentience:** How does the place feel? Warm? Cold? Peaceful? Bustling?

5. **Clairvoyance:** What colors or shapes do you see in your mind's eye? Are there lines? Curves? A dominant color?

6. **Clairaudience:** Do you hear any sounds associated with the place? Waves? Wind? Traffic?

7. **Claircognizance:** Do you just know something about it? "It's outdoors." "There's water."

8. **Sketch and Record.** Write down and sketch everything that comes through, no matter how small or strange it seems.

9. **Compare and Validate.** After the time is up, connect with your friend and have them show you the image. Compare your notes. You will be amazed at how often your impressions, even if not a perfect picture, align with the energy and content of the target image.

This practice, repeated over time, builds incredible trust in your ability to send your awareness beyond the confines of your physical senses. It is the conscious and joyful application of a skill I once had to use just to know if it was safe to walk down the hall.

Remember, the goal of these practices is not to escape your life, but to more fully inhabit it. It is to understand, through direct experience, that you are a magnificent, multi-dimensional soul. The ability to leave your body is not a symptom of your brokenness; it is definitive proof of your infinite and unbreakable spirit. You have not just survived; you have learned to fly.

CHAPTER TWENTY

The Alchemist's Life: Integrating Your Gifts

The little girl who learned to see in the dark did not do so to become a psychic. She did it to survive. She learned to read the subtle shifts of energy in a room, to feel the unspoken emotions of others, and to know what was coming, not because she was seeking a spiritual gift, but because she was desperately searching for a safe place to stand.

If your story is anything like mine, then your intuitive abilities were born in a similar crucible. They were not a party trick; they were a shield, a compass, a whispered secret that kept you safe. The journey we have taken together in this book has been about alchemy—the sacred act of taking that raw, reactive survival mechanism and consciously transforming it into a beautiful, intentional, and sacred gift.

But what happens now? What does it look like to walk through the world not as a survivor in a constant state of high alert, but as a sovereign, intuitive being? How do we integrate these profound gifts into the messy, beautiful, and often very ordinary fabric of our daily lives?

This is not a finish line. There is no final exam, no graduation ceremony from the school of the soul. The alchemist's life is a practice, a gentle unfolding, a daily choice to listen to the quiet whisper of your spirit over the loud clamor of the world. It is about learning to trust the compass you were given and allowing it to guide you, not just in moments of ceremony, but in the sacred ordinary of your life. In this final chapter, we will explore how to walk this path with grace, integrity, and a deep, abiding love for the brilliant soul you have become.

Trusting Your Intuition:
The Sacred Ordinary

When I first began to consciously embrace my abilities, I think I expected my intuition to arrive like a bolt of lightning, delivering grand, cinematic pronouncements about the future. But that is rarely how it works. The language of spirit is subtle. It speaks in nudges, in quiet feelings, in the song that gets stuck in your head, in the sudden urge to call a friend.

Integrating your gifts into your daily life is about learning to honor these small, sacred nudges. It's about inviting your intuition to the table when you're deciding what to eat for lunch, which route to take to work, or whether to say yes or no to a social invitation. It's in these small, low-stakes decisions that you build the muscle of intuitive trust.

In my own life, my intuition is my most trusted business partner. As a marketing professional, I can analyze data and create strategies, but my greatest successes have always come when I've listened to a claircognizant "knowing" about which creative direction to take, or when my clairsentience has allowed me to truly feel and understand the needs of an audience. It guides me as a mother, giving me a gut feeling when one of my sons needs a quiet conversation, even when he says he's fine. It is a constant, loving presence, a silent collaborator in the art of living.

EXERCISE 1: THE DAILY COMPASS

This is a practice to shift your intuition from something you "do" in meditation to something you "are" in the world.

1. **Set a Morning Intention.** As you start your day, perhaps as you sip your morning coffee or tea, take a quiet moment. Close your eyes, take a breath, and set a simple intention: "Today, I will pay attention to my intuitive nudges. I invite my spirit to be my compass." That's it. You are simply opening the door.

2. **Notice the Nudges Throughout Your Day.** As you move through your day, practice noticing the subtle ways your intuition speaks to you, without judgment.

3. **Clairsentience:** You walk into a meeting and your stomach tightens. Just notice it. You're talking to a friend and you feel a sudden wave of warmth and joy. Notice that, too.

4. **Clairvoyance:** You're thinking about a project and a random image of a flower pops into your mind. Don't dismiss it. Just make a mental note.

5. **Clairaudience:** You're driving and a specific song comes on the radio with lyrics that seem to answer a question you've been pondering. Acknowledge the synchronicity.

6. **Claircognizance:** You suddenly have the unshakeable urge to take the scenic route home.

7. **Evening Reflection** (Without Judgment). Before you go to sleep, take five minutes with a journal. Look back on your day and write down any of the nudges you noticed. The key here is zero

judgment. It doesn't matter if you followed the nudge or not. It doesn't matter if it "made sense." The goal is not to get a perfect score. The goal is simply to practice recognizing the language. The more you notice, the louder and clearer the voice of your intuition will become.

The Ethics of Being Psychic:
The Sacred Responsibility

As your intuitive senses become stronger, you will begin to perceive information about other people. You will feel their pain, sense their secrets, and sometimes, you will know things about them that they have not consciously shared. This is a sacred and profound responsibility.

The little girl who was violated in the dark learned the paramount importance of sovereignty and consent. My body and my energy were not respected. As intuitive adults, we must become fierce and loving guardians of this principle, both for ourselves and for others. Our gifts must never, ever be used to violate another person's energetic or emotional privacy.

This is not about a list of rigid rules, but about a heart-centered orientation of service and respect. When I was channeling the portraits, the spirits of the children taught me everything I needed to know about ethics. They communicated with a purity of love that was breathtaking. Their only intention was to bring comfort and healing to their families. This became my own North Star. Before I share any information, I always ask: "Is this for the highest good of all? Is this born of love? Is this in service to healing?"

The Three Pillars of Intuitive Ethics

1. **Permission is Paramount.** You do not have the right to "read" someone without their explicit permission. Just because you can sense their energy does not mean you should. Peeking into someone's energetic field without their consent is the psychic equivalent of reading their diary. Always ask. If a friend is telling you about a problem, you can gently ask, "Would you be open to hearing an intuitive hit I'm getting about this?" Respect their "no" as much as their "yes."

2. **Serve, Don't Show Off.** Your gifts are not for proving you are right or for impressing others. They are for service. I learned this most profoundly when I made the decision to offer the Angel Portraits for free. My soul knew that putting a price on that sacred exchange would have tainted it with ego. The goal is not to be the most "gifted" psychic; the goal is to be the clearest and most loving channel for whatever healing wishes to come through you.

3. **Empower, Don't Predict.** The future is not a fixed point. It is a fluid dance of energy and free will. A true spiritual guide does not disempower someone by handing them a rigid prediction of their future. Instead, they empower them by illuminating the energies and potentials of the present moment, allowing them to make their own highest choices. Instead of saying, "You will get the job," you can say, "The energy around this job opportunity feels expansive and aligned with your growth." The first is a prediction; the second is empowerment.

Finding Your Purpose:
The Alchemist's Legacy

We have arrived at the end of this book, but the true beginning of your journey. You have walked with me through the darkest rooms of my past. You have sat with me in the sanctuary of my present. You have learned the science and the practice of the alchemy that turned my greatest wounds into my most sacred gifts.

Now, it is time to fully claim your own.

The world may have told you that your trauma was a source of shame, a story to be hidden, a part of you that is broken. I am here to tell you that this is the greatest lie you have ever been told. Your trauma is the signature of your soul's curriculum on this earth. It is the specific, tailor-made pressure that was required to form the diamond of your unique spirit. You are not broken. You are a specialist.

The little girl who felt invisible became a woman who could see the unseen. The little girl who was never heard became a woman who could hear the whispers of spirit. The little girl who was starving for love became a woman who could serve as a conduit for a love that transcends death itself.

Your story has its own sacred poetry. Your deepest wounds have forged your greatest strengths. The final step in this alchemical process is to recognize that gift and to offer it back to the world in service.

EXERCISE 2: THE GOLDEN THREAD

This final exercise is a reflection to help you identify the golden thread that weaves through your own life, connecting your pain to your purpose. Take your time with these questions in your journal.

1. **Identify the Core Wound.** Go back to the heart of your childhood pain. What was the central feeling? Was it the feeling of being unseen? Unheard? Unsafe? Abandoned? Powerless? Write it down.
2. **Identify the Brilliant Adaptation.** Now, what specific skill did you have to develop to survive that feeling? If you felt unseen, did you become a masterful observer of others? If you felt unheard, did you become an incredibly deep listener? If you felt unsafe, did you develop a hyper-attuned sense of your environment?
3. **Identify the Sacred Gift.** Look at that skill you developed. How can that brilliant adaptation, now that you are safe, be consciously used as a sacred gift in service to others?

The masterful observer can become a clairvoyant who sees the truth for others.

The deep listener can become a clairaudient who hears the guidance others need.

The hyper-attuned empath can become a clairsentient who feels and validates the emotions of others, helping them to heal.

Look at the golden thread that connects your wound to your gift. This is the heart of your purpose. This is your unique medicine for the world.

PART V

The Alchemist's Sanctuary

You have gathered your tools. You have walked through the science of your own sacred brain and built the foundations of your inner sanctuary. You now understand the language of spirit, the practice of protection, and the pathways of the four clairs.

But the true alchemy happens not in the knowing, but in the being. A toolkit is for building, but a sanctuary is for communion.

Now, I want to take you by the hand and walk with you into that sacred space. This section offers you a series of guided meditations—the keys to the sanctuary's quietest, most holy rooms. To bring these journeys to life, I warmly invite you to record them in your own voice, letting the sound of your own words become a powerful, personal anchor. Or, if you prefer, you can find my voice waiting for you in the audiobook version, ready to walk with you personally.

These are not just moments of stillness; they are active explorations into the heart of your own spirit. They are your invitations to explore, trust, and fully embody your own sacred gift.

MEDITATION ONE

The Root and the Star:
A Foundational Grounding Meditation

(Soft, gentle music can be played in the background. Pacing should be slow, with pauses where indicated by ⧗)

Hello, dear friend. Welcome.

Welcome to this sacred time, just for you. Find a space where you can be undisturbed, where you feel safe and supported. You can sit comfortably in a chair, with your feet flat on the floor, or lie down, allowing your body to be fully held.

Gently, when you're ready, allow your eyes to close.

Let us begin by arriving. Just ⧗ arriving. Letting go of the day, the to-do lists, the worries. Give yourself this gift of presence.

As you settle in, you might notice the watchman in your mind's watchtower. The part of you that is always on alert, always scanning, always listening. Let's just acknowledge him. We can gently say to him, "Thank you for protecting me. But in this moment, in this sacred space, you can come down from the tower. You can rest. For right now ⧖ all is well."

Bring your awareness to your breath. Just notice it, without trying to change it. Feel the air entering your body ⧖ and feel the tension leaving with each exhale.

Take a deep breath. Breathe into the base of your spine. Exhale out of the top of your head.

⧖

Now, let us begin the work of our sanctuary.

I want you to imagine a brilliant, beautiful star of divine light, shining high above you. A pure, unconditional, loving light. This is the "Star" of your own spirit, your connection to the all-that-is.

On your next inhale, I want you to imagine drawing this beautiful, liquid-gold light down through the crown of your head. Feel it travel down, a warm, healing stream ⧖ all the way down your neck ⧖ your chest ⧖ your belly ⧖ all the way down until it pools at the very base of your spine. Feel it gather there, a warm, radiant sun at the base of your being.

Hold it for just a moment.

And now, as you exhale, imagine that light traveling up your spine, a gentle, shimmering current ⧗ up ⧗ up ⧗ all the way up, until it flows out the very top of your head in a soft, beautiful fountain of light, cascading all around you.

Let's do this again.

Inhale, drawing that divine "Star" light down from the heavens ⧗ down ⧗ down ⧗ all the way to the "Root" at the base of your spine. Let it gather.

⧗

Exhale, and send that light flowing all the way back up your spine ⧗ out through your crown ⧗ creating a beautiful, protective aura of light all around you.

⧗

Continue this breath. Inhaling light down to your Root. Exhaling light up and out from your Star. With every breath, this column of light within you grows stronger, clearer, and brighter. You are building your inner sanctuary, right now, with your own breath. You are safe. You are held.

⧗

Now, as you continue this gentle, rhythmic breathing, I want you to allow your awareness to drift. Let's use that visionary skill you've always had.

Allow a soft, hazy blue mist to gather in your mind's eye ⧗ like the memory of your sacred space. I could be somewhere you've been before, somewhere you'll visit in the future, or simply a place you've made up in your mind's eye. Wherever it may be it is the exact place for you. It's peaceful here. Quiet.

As you breathe, this gentle mist begins to part ⌛ and you find yourself standing at the edge of a winding path, perhaps in a tunnel of trees, or on a sandy beach with tall sea grass carving a winding path, or a mountain meadow filled with the scent of fresh flowers.. The light is soft, possibly filtering through the leaves in golden patterns, or shifting brilliance through white puffy clouds. You can smell the rich, damp earth, salt in the air, or fresh floral fragrance ⌛ or the scent of pine and ancient stone. Just allow these scents to tickle your nose.

⌛

You feel a pull to walk this path. You are completely safe here. This is your own inner world.

You walk ⌛ and as you do, you notice the sounds. The gentle whisper of the wind through the leaves ⌛ a distant bird… the rhythmic sounds of rolling waves or a trickling brook, along with the soft sound of your own footsteps on the path.

Your path begins to open up ⌛ and you step out into a small, secret clearing. A round, green meadow, high on the mountain. The grass is soft ⌛ and you have the sudden urge to take off your shoes. You do.

And you feel it ⌛ just as you did as a child. The profound feeling of the cool, damp earth beneath your feet. The blades of grass tickling your toes. You are connected. You are real. You are here.

⌛

I want you to stand in the center of this sacred place. This is your sanctuary. Your place of power.

Feel that connection to the earth ⌛ and now, let's deepen it.

From the soles of your feet ⌛ and from that beautiful "Root" of light at the base of your spine ⌛ I want you to imagine roots beginning to grow. Just like a beautiful majestic tree.

Feel them ⌛ thick, strong, energetic roots ⌛ extending down from your body. Feel them pushing down ⌛ down ⌛ easily, effortlessly ⌛ past the topsoil ⌛ past the cool, dark rock ⌛

Deeper and deeper they go ⌛ spreading wide ⌛ anchoring you. Feel them plunging into the very heart of the planet ⌛ down into the molten, crystalline core of the Earth.

⌛

Feel your roots wrap themselves securely around this glowing, nurturing core. And as they do ⌛ you feel a profound sense of belonging. A wave of unconditional love and stability flows up from the Earth.

This is the Earth's "knowing."

It flows up your roots ⌛ and you hear the whisper of its truth. You hear: "I hold you. I see you. You are not alone. You have always been safe with me. Your walk on this earth is sacred. You belong here."

Feel that nurturing energy ⌛ that absolute stability ⌛ flow up into your feet ⧖ your legs ⧖ filling your entire lower body with a deep, unshakable peace. You are anchored. You are held. Nothing can move you. You are home.

⧖

Now ⧖ as your roots drink deep from the nurturing Earth ⧖ bring your awareness back to your body. You are no longer just standing here. You are this anchor. You are becoming the tree.

Feel your spine ⧖ strong, straight, and true ⧖ the trunk of your being.

Feel your skin ⧖ like strong, protective bark, holding your sacred energy within.

And from your heart ⧖ from your shoulders ⧖ from the crown of your head ⧖ feel yourself begin to reach up.

Just as your roots grew down ⧖ your branches now grow up.

Feel them extending ⧖ reaching for the sky ⧖ past the mountain peaks ⧖ past the soft, white clouds ⧖

Higher and higher they reach ⧖ spreading out wide ⧖ up into the hazy blue of the sky ⧖ and beyond ⧖ into the deep, star-dusted velvet of the cosmos.

You are reaching for the "Star." You are reaching for the heavens.

⧖

And as your branches touch the sky ⧖ you feel a new connection. A

155

new light.

The light of a billion stars ⧗ the knowledge of the universe ⧗ begins to flow into your branches. It is not knowledge as words or facts ⧗ it is knowledge as feeling. As light. As frequency.

You feel the frequencies of peace ⧗ of infinite wisdom ⧗ of creation ⧗ of unconditional love.

You feel the truth of your own soul ⧗ that you are not small ⧗ that you are not broken ⧗ that you are an infinite, magnificent being of light.

You are a channel. You are an alchemist.

⧗

Take a long moment now ⧗ just to be this tree.

You are the Alchemist's Tree.

Your roots are drinking deep from the "Root" of the Earth ⧗ receiving the unconditional love, nurturing, and "knowing" of your sacred walk.

Your branches are reaching high into the "Star" ⧗ receiving the infinite wisdom, light, and knowledge of the universe.

You are the bridge between Earth and Sky. You are the anchor and the antenna. The sacred and the solid.

Feel the perfect balance of this. The Earth's energy flows up your trunk ⧗ the Star's energy flows down your trunk ⧗ and they meet in the center of your being ⧗ in your heart.

Feel them swirl together ⧗ Earth and Sky ⧗ Root and Star.

This is your alchemy. This is your divine power. This is the unshakeable peace of your true self.

⧗

Stay here ⧗ rooted and reaching ⧗ for as long as you wish. There is nothing to do. Nothing to fix. Only to be.

Your watchman is fast asleep at the base of your trunk, finally at peace.

You are safe. You are whole. You are ⧗ you.

⧗

⧗

Now ⧗ with a deep sense of gratitude ⧗ it is time to integrate this.

Let us first thank the heavens, the Star. Feel your branches gently begin to retract ⧗ bringing all of that cosmic wisdom, all of that starlight, with you ⧗ drawing it back ⧗ back ⧗ down into the crown of your head ⧗ and into your heart.

Now, let us thank the Earth, the Root. Feel your roots gently begin to retract ⧗ bringing all of that nurturing love, all of that "knowing," with you ⧗ drawing it back ⧗ back ⧗ up into the soles of your feet ⧗ and into your heart.

Feel that power ⧗ that knowing ⧗ that light ⧗ now held securely within the sanctuary of your own heart.

You are not leaving the tree behind. You are the tree. You are bringing its strength with you.

⧗

Gently, bring your awareness back to your human body, resting in this room. Feel the solid ground beneath your feet ⧗ the chair or floor beneath you.

But know that your roots are still there, just beneath the surface, ready at any moment. Know that your star-connection is still there, just above your crown, always waiting.

Your sanctuary is built. Your channel is clear.

Slowly ⧗ gently ⧗ begin to bring small movements back to your body. Wiggle your fingers ⧗ and your toes. Maybe roll your shoulders, or gently stretch your neck.

And when you are ready, and only when you are ready ⧗ you may open your eyes.

⧗

Welcome back, alchemist.

You have stepped back into the world, not as you left it ⧗ but as the anchor. As the channel. Take this feeling of unshakeable peace with you. You are stepping back into your divine power. You are ready to use your sacred gifts. You are home.

The Garden of the Senses: A Meditation to Meet Your Clairs

(Soft, gentle music can be played in the background. Pacing should be slow, with pauses where indicated by ⧗)

Hello again, dear alchemist. Welcome to your own sacred space.

Find a position that feels like a true sanctuary for your body. Sitting, with your spine tall and your feet firmly on the earth, or lying down, feeling every part of you held and supported.

And when you feel ready, gently allow your eyes to close.

Let's begin by simply arriving. Releasing the day ⧗ the noise ⧗ the expectations. Just be here, in this quiet, protected room you are building inside yourself.

Let's call in that beautiful, divine light. Imagine a brilliant, loving star of pure, white-gold light shining high above you ⧗ a star of your own divine essence.

On your next inhale, I want you to draw this starlight down ⧗

breathing it in through the crown of your head. Feel this liquid light travel down your body ⏳ a warm, healing stream ⏳ all the way down ⏳ down ⏳ until it pools like a radiant, warm sun at the very base of your spine.

Hold it there, at your root.

And as you exhale, imagine this light flowing up your spine ⏳ a strong, clear current ⏳ up through your heart ⏳ your throat ⏳ and out the top of your head in a brilliant, shimmering fountain ⏳ cascading down and all around you, forming that beautiful bubble of light, your sacred sanctuary.

Let's do this again, building our container.

Inhale ⏳ drawing that starlight down ⏳ down ⏳ down to the base of your spine. Feel it gather, warm and safe.

⏳

Exhale ⏳ sending that light all the way up ⏳ and out ⏳ reinforcing your bubble of light. You are safe. You are sovereign. You are protected.

⏳

Just continue this breath ⏳ this "Fountain of Light" ⏳ breathing in the heavens, breathing out your sanctuary. With every breath, the watchman in your mind's watchtower feels safer. He sees the golden light around you. He knows that for this moment, in this breath, all is well. He can finally rest.

⏳

Now, from this place of safety, I want you to imagine a new space appearing in your mind's eye.

Perhaps a hazy, blue mountain mist gathers around you ⧗ as it parts, it reveals something unexpected.

You find yourself standing before an old, high wall, covered in soft, green ivy. And in this wall, there is a small, wooden gate. It feels familiar, like a place you knew as a child ⧗ a place you built in your mind to be safe.

You reach for the handle, and the gate opens with a soft, welcoming sound.

You step through ⧗ and a feeling of profound relief washes over you, just like opening your first sketchbook. You are in a garden. Your own secret, sacred garden.

⧗

This is your soul's sanctuary. It is a world you can control. A world where you are sovereign. Take a moment to just ⧗ be here.

What does it look like? ⧗ What can you smell? Is it the scent of roses ⧗ or damp earth ⧗ or the sea? ⧗ The light here is soft and kind. The air is still and peaceful. You are completely and totally safe.

⧗

This is the garden of your senses ⧗ the garden of your soul's senses. And we are here to discover your native language.

First, let's explore Clairsentience ⧖ "Clear Feeling."

You begin to walk on a soft, mossy path. As you walk, your gaze is drawn to a small, smooth stone beside the path, warmed by a ray of light.

I invite you to bend and pick it up.

Feel it in the palm of your hand. Notice its physical properties ⧖ Is it heavy, or light? Is it perfectly smooth, or does it have a texture? ⧖ Notice its temperature.

Now, I want you to go deeper. Gently close your hand around the stone ⧖ and set the intention to feel its story. To feel its energy.

⧖

Just be open. What is the first feeling that comes to you? Is it a feeling of joy? ⧖ A feeling of stillness? ⧖ A feeling of great age and wisdom? Does it carry an echo of sadness ⧖ or a feeling of deep, abiding peace?

You are not making this up. You are reading with your hands, with your heart. This is the language of the empath, your brilliant adaptation, now used as a sacred tool. You are feeling the unseen.

There is no right or wrong. Just acknowledge the feeling. This is Clairsentience. Gently, you can place the stone back down, giving thanks for its story.

Now, let's explore Clairvoyance ⌛ "Clear Seeing."

You continue on the path, and it opens into a quiet, secluded alcove. Here, the grass is lush and green, and in the center is a patch of rich, dark earth. You see a single plant, with a bud that is tightly closed.

This is a flower that is waiting just for you. It will bloom only for your inner eye.

I want you to soften your gaze. Look at this bud not with your physical eyes, but with your "mind's eye" ⌛ the way you would see a face in your sketchbook before the pencil even touched the paper.

⌛

Hold the intention to see it bloom. And just ⌛ watch.

⌛

What color is it? ⌛ Is it a soft, gentle pink ⌛ or a brilliant, electric blue ⌛ or a deep, royal purple? ⌛ Trust the very first flash of color that comes to you. ⌛ Look closer. See the shape of its petals. Are they wide and open, or delicate and pointed? Can you see the tiny flecks of light on its surface? ⌛ The details?

You are seeing with your soul. The image is real. This is the language of the visionary. This is Clairvoyance. Take a moment to thank this beautiful flower for revealing itself to you.

Now, let's explore Clairaudience ⧗ "Clear Hearing."

You leave the alcove and find yourself on a small, gentle hill at the center of your garden. A soft, warm breeze begins to move around you, rustling the leaves of a nearby willow tree.

I want you to stop ⧗ and just ⧗ listen.

At first, you hear the physical sounds ⧗ the leaves ⧗ a distant bird ⧗ the sound of your own breath. Acknowledge them.

⧗

Now, listen a little deeper, beneath those sounds. You may hear the static of your own mind ⧗ the to-do lists, the worries. The chatter of the watchman. Acknowledge this too, and just let it be, like a passing cloud.

⧗

Now, I want you to listen even deeper. Listen to the silence ⧗ the space between the sounds. Set the intention to hear the song of the wind. To hear the whisper beneath the silence.

⧗

What do you hear? It is likely not a loud, booming voice. It is a whisper. It might be a single word ⧗ like "Peace" ⧗ or "Listen" ⧗ or "Home." It might be a note of music ⧗ or a soft, loving hum. It might be that "symphony of abdication" you once heard, now transformed into a symphony of love ⧗ a feeling of pure, loving presence, translated by your soul into sound.

Be still ⧗ and just ⧗ receive. ⧗ This is the language of the quiet listener. This is Clairaudience. Give thanks for the message of the wind.

⧗

Finally, let's explore Claircognizance ⧗ "Clear Knowing."

You come down from the hill. And you feel a gentle, inner thirst ⧗ a longing for the truth. You know, with a sudden certainty, that somewhere in this sacred garden ⧗ there is a hidden spring of pure, clear knowing.

But you will not find it with your eyes, or your ears, or your hands. You will find it with your gut. With your bones.

⧗

Stand still. Take a deep breath. Do not look. Do not listen. Just ⧗ ask in your mind. "Where is the spring of my truth?"

⧗

Now, let them go. Let go of the question. Let go of the "trying." And just wait for the answer. It will not be a voice. It will be a pull. A sudden, unshakeable, "cold, heavy knowing" ⧗ a feeling that arrives without reason, that simply settles in your stomach. You will just know which way to turn.

⧗

Trust it. Trust that first, instantaneous flash of knowing. Now ⧗ follow it. Turn in the direction your gut told you. Walk down that path. You walk with certainty ⧗ past a grove of silver birches ⧗ around a bend ⧗ And there it is.

⧗

A small, quiet spring, bubbling up from the earth, the water so clear it shimmers like crystal. This is your truth. This is your unshakable, inner compass. You knelt and waited for your mother out of this same knowing. But here, in this garden, the knowing is not a warning of pain. It is a guide to your deepest wisdom. This is the language of the soul. This is Claircognizance.

⧗

Take a moment now, by this spring of truth. Reflect on your journey through this garden. The feeling of the stone. The sight of the flower. The sound of the wind. The knowing of the path.

Which one felt most natural to you? Which one felt like ⧗ coming home? You may have felt a strong pull to one ⧗ or a gentle hum in all four. There is no "right" way. There is only your way. This is your soul's native language. Your sacred gift, revealed.

⧗

Now, it is time to return, to bring this knowing back with you. Give thanks to your sacred garden. Give thanks to the spring, the wind, the flower, the stone. Know that this gate is always here for you. You can return at any time.

You turn and walk back to the gate, step through, and gently close it behind you.

⧗

Bring your awareness back to your breath. That Fountain of Light. Inhaling the starlight down to your root ⧗ Exhaling that fountain of light up and out from your crown.

Bring your awareness back to your physical body, in this room. Feel the solid surface beneath you, holding you. Know that you are anchored. You are safe. But you are returning with something new.

You are stepping back into the world with the clear knowing of your soul's native language. You are ready to listen ⧗ to see ⧗ to feel ⧗ to know.

⧗

Gently, begin to bring small movements back to your body. Wiggle your fingers, and your toes. Maybe roll your shoulders, or nod your head.

And when you feel fully present, anchored in your power ⧗ you may open your eyes.

Welcome back, alchemist. Welcome back to your sacred gifts.

The Kintsugi Heart:
A Meditation for Alchemizing Your Wound

(Soft, gentle, and calming music can be played in the background. Pacing should be slow, with pauses where indicated by ⧗)

Hello, dear alchemist. Welcome.

There is a Japanese art form called kintsugi, where broken pottery is repaired by mending the cracks with lacquer mixed with powdered gold. The philosophy is that the piece is more beautiful and valuable because it has been broken. The scars are not something to be hidden; they are the most beautiful part of the object's history, a testament to its resilience.

Find your comfortable space, where you can feel completely at ease, safe, and supported. Whether you're sitting or lying down, allow your body to relax deeply into its support.

And when you're ready, gently allow your eyes to close.

Let us begin by just being. Letting go of any expectations, any worries, any need to do anything right now. This time is for your heart.

Bring your awareness to your breath. Feel it flowing in, nourishing every cell. Feel it flowing out, releasing any tension, any holding. Each breath is an act of presence.

⧖

Now, let's build our beautiful sanctuary, our container of sacred light.

Imagine that brilliant, loving star of pure, white-gold divine light shining high above you ⧖ your own connection to infinite love and wisdom.

On your next inhale, draw this starlight down through the crown of your head ⧖ a warm, healing stream ⧖ all the way down your neck ⧖ your chest ⧖ your belly ⧖ until it pools like a radiant, gentle sun at the very base of your spine. Feel it gather there, a warm, protective energy.

Hold it there, at your root.

And now, as you exhale, imagine that light flowing up your spine ⧖ a clear, strong current ⧖ up through your heart ⧖ your throat ⧖ and out the top of your head in a soft, shimmering fountain ⧖ cascading down and all around you, forming a resilient, beautiful bubble of pure, golden light. This is your personal sanctuary.

⧖

Continue this beautiful breath. Inhaling the divine "Star" light down to your root. Exhaling this light up and out, reinforcing your protective bubble. With every breath, you are creating a sacred, impenetrable space of love and safety around you. You are truly safe. You are truly sovereign.

⧗

The watchman in your mind's tower can now truly rest. He sees your golden bubble. He feels the peace within. He knows you are held. He knows you are protected.

⧗

Now, in the center of this golden bubble, I want you to visualize your heart. See it glowing, perhaps with a soft, radiant light. This is your Kintsugi Heart.

We are here today for the heart of the alchemist's work: to lovingly acknowledge and embrace the golden thread that weaves through your life, connecting your deepest wound to your most profound gift.

There is no need to relive any pain. We are simply going to offer love.

⧗

From the safety of your golden sanctuary, I want you to gently recall the core wound from your childhood. Not the events themselves, but the feeling that was at its center.

Was it the feeling of being unseen? ⧗ unheard? ⧗ unsafe? ⧗ abandoned? ⧗ powerless?

Just allow that feeling to surface gently, like a wisp of mist in your golden bubble. Do not judge it. Do not analyze it. Just feel it. And send it love.

⧗

Now, with compassion in your heart, I want you to visualize the younger version of you who held that feeling. The little girl ⧗ or the little boy ⧗ who experienced that core wound.

See them now, in your mind's eye. They might be small. They might look scared, or lonely, or lost. They might be in a shadowy corner, or looking out from behind a curtain.

You, the adult, loving alchemist that you are today, are completely safe in your golden bubble. And you are reaching out to them from this place of immense strength and love.

⧗

Gently, tenderly, invite them to step forward. Not into your bubble, unless they feel ready, but into a soft, loving light near your bubble. A light that you have created, just for them.

⧗

See them. Acknowledge them. Look into their eyes, not with pity, but with profound recognition and love. This is the child who brilliantly adapted. This is the child who survived. This is the child who laid the foundation for the magnificent, intuitive being you are today.

⧗

Now, from your Kintsugi Heart, filled with that beautiful, healing, white-gold light, I want you to extend a beam of pure, unconditional love to that child.

See this golden light flowing from your heart ⧗ gently enveloping them. Imagine yourself saying to them, silently, or softly aloud if you wish:

"I see you. I hear you. I am here now. And you are safe. We are safe." "I know you were unseen ⧗ unheard ⧗ unsafe ⧗ abandoned ⧗ powerless. But you were so brave. You survived. You adapted."

⧗

Allow that golden light from your heart to fill their small form. See any shadows around them begin to dissipate as they are bathed in your loving presence.

Imagine you are holding their hand, or gently putting an arm around them. They are not alone anymore. You, the powerful adult, are here.

⧗

Now, speak to them about their brilliant adaptation.

"That skill you developed to survive ⧗ that hyper-sensitivity ⧗ that deep listening ⧗ that knowing ⧗ that seeing beyond ⧗ that was not a flaw. That was a sacred gift being forged. That was your alchemy."

"You are not broken, little one. You were becoming a specialist. A masterpiece. And your scars ⧗ they are not something to be hidden. They are the most beautiful part of your story. The gold that fills them is the proof of your resilience."

🏳

Take a moment to just sit with this truth. You, the adult, are meeting the child. And you are not asking them to heal you. You are simply offering them the love, the safety, and the validation they so desperately needed then, and that you can provide now.

Feel their presence. Perhaps they offer you a small smile. Perhaps you feel a softening in your own chest. This is integration. This is healing.

🏳

Now, from this place of deep love and connection, I want you to envision a beautiful, golden thread. This is your golden thread.

See it emerging from the heart of that younger you 🏳 a shimmering, unbreakable strand of light. And see it connecting directly to your Kintsugi Heart, the heart of the powerful, intuitive adult you are today.

🏳

Feel the continuous flow of love and wisdom moving along this thread. From the depth of your past experience, to the strength of your present wisdom.

This golden thread is the proof that your deepest wound has, indeed, become your most profound source of power. It is not something to forget, or erase, but to honor. It is the gold that fills the cracks.

⧗

You are now the living embodiment of Kintsugi. More beautiful, more valuable, and more powerful because of your journey.

Hold this truth in your heart.

⧗

With immense gratitude for your brave younger self, and for the wisdom you have retrieved, it is time to gently integrate.

Thank that younger version of you. Let them know they can always return to this sacred space, to this light, whenever they need to feel safe and loved. They are now, and always will be, safe within your Kintsugi Heart.

You are not leaving them. You are holding them, lovingly, within you.

⧗

Bring your awareness back to your breath. That beautiful Fountain of Light, flowing in and out. Feel your protective golden bubble around you, strong and secure.

Feel your body resting in this room, fully present, fully held.

Your heart feels lighter. Your spirit feels stronger. You have completed a profound act of alchemy. You have mended your heart with gold.

Gently, begin to bring small movements back to your body. Wiggle your fingers and your toes. Maybe roll your shoulders, or gently stretch your neck.

And when you feel fully present, anchored in this golden, healed power, you may open your eyes.

Welcome back, alchemist.

You carry the strength of your past, transformed into the gold of your present. You are whole. You are powerful. You are ready to offer your magnificent, resilient, and brilliant soul to the world. You are home.

The Quiet Room:
A Meditation to Meet Your Guide

(Soft, gentle, and peaceful music can be played in the background. Pacing should be slow, with pauses where indicated by ⧗)

Hello, my dear friend. Welcome back to this sacred, quiet space you have carved out just for yourself.

Find your comfortable, safe position. A chair where your feet can feel the earth, or lying down where your body can be completely and utterly held.

And when you feel ready, gently allow your eyes to close.

Let us begin by arriving. Just arriving. Setting down the day, the week, the worries ⧗ like a heavy bag by the door. You can pick it up later if you choose, but for now, you are free.

⧗

Bring your awareness to your breath. That simple, holy act of breathing. Feel the air enter your body ⧗ and feel the tension, the noise, the static, just ⏳ dissolve on the exhale. You are here. You are present. You are safe.

⏳

Now, let us build our beautiful, strong container.

I want you to imagine that brilliant, loving star of pure, white-gold light shining high above you ⏳ your own divine connection.

On your next inhale, draw this liquid starlight down ⏳ down through the crown of your head ⏳ a warm, healing stream ⏳ down, down, all the way to the very base of your spine. Feel it pool there, a radiant, steady sun at your root.

Hold it for just a moment.

And now, as you exhale, imagine that light flowing up your spine ⏳ a strong, clear current ⏳ up through your heart ⏳ your throat ⏳ and out the top of your head in a brilliant, shimmering fountain ⏳ cascading down and all around you, forming a beautiful, resilient bubble of pure, protective, golden light.

⏳

Let's do this again, strengthening our sanctuary.

Inhale ⏳ drawing that divine "Star" light down ⏳ all the way to your root. Feel it.

⏳

Exhale ⌛ sending that light all the way back up ⌛ and out ⌛ reinforcing this sacred, golden bubble. This is your personal, sovereign space. You are in complete control. Only energies of the highest love and for your highest good may enter.

The watchman in your mind's tower ⌛ he can feel this profound safety. He can see the golden walls of this sanctuary you have built. You can feel him take a deep breath, and for the first time, perhaps, he comes down from his post. He knows that in this space, in this moment ⌛ all is well.

⌛

Now, from within this beautiful, golden bubble ⌛ I want you to imagine a new space. You are going to create, with your intention, a "quiet room." A room just for you.

What does it look like? ⌛ It doesn't have to be grand. Perhaps it's that cozy room you always dreamed of as a child. Perhaps it's a room from your granny's house, filled with the smell of biscuits. Perhaps it's a simple, elegant space with a high ceiling, filled with soft, white light. Or maybe it's a small, round room, like the inside of a jewel.

This is your inner sanctuary. You are the architect.

⌛

In the center of this room, I want you to place the most comfortable chair you can imagine. A chair that feels like a hug. A chair that feels like home. Go ahead and take a seat in this chair. Feel how it supports you. How it holds you. The light in this room is soft and kind. The temperature is perfect. The silence here is not the terrifying silence of waiting ⧖ it is the peaceful, holy silence of knowing.

This is your sacred meeting place.

⧖

You are not, and have never been, alone. Your whole life, even in the darkest, most terrifying moments, you have been surrounded by a "silent congregation" of loving, wise, and patient souls. Guides, angels, ancestors ⧖ who have been walking with you, whispering encouragement, holding a light for you.

You've been listening in the dark your whole life ⧖ and you have become a master at it. Now, we are just going to practice listening in the light.

⧖

From your comfortable chair, in your safe, quiet room ⧖ I want you to set a simple, gentle intention. You can say it in your mind, or in your heart.

"I am here, in love and in safety. I now invite my highest, wisest, and most loving spirit guide ⧖ the one who is most appropriate for my highest good to connect with me now ⧖ I invite you to gently make your presence known. I am open to feeling your love. I am ready to know your signature."

⧖

That is all. The invitation is sent. There is nothing to force. Nothing to strain for. You are not trying to see or hear anything. You are simply

⏳ sitting. In a state of open, loving, curious awareness. You are the sensitive radio, your dial tuned to the frequency of pure love. You are just ⏳ listening.

⏳

Just be still ⏳ and feel. How does the energy in the room shift? Even subtly?

⏳

Do you suddenly feel a warmth on one side of your body? A gentle tingle in your hands, or at the crown of your head? ⏳ Do you feel a sudden, profound wave of peace wash over you ⏳ a feeling of "all is well" that is so deep, you know it is not just your own? ⏳ This is a signature.

⏳

Perhaps you feel something else. A sudden, unshakable sense of age and wisdom ⏳ like being in the presence of an ancient, loving grandparent. Or perhaps a feeling of light, bubbly joy ⏳ a sense of humor, even. This is a signature.

⏳

Pay attention to your inner senses. You might get a fleeting image in your mind's eye ⏳ not a full person, but perhaps a color ⏳ a soft, deep blue, or a gentle rose pink. You might "hear" a single word in your mind ⏳ like "Welcome" ⏳ or "Peace" ⏳ or "Always." You might just know, with that claircognizant certainty, that settles in your bones ⏳ "I am here."

⧗

Do not doubt what you get. However subtle it is ⧗ that is it. That is their "hello." That is their calling card. This is the "signature of love" that you are learning to recognize. For years, you were trained to feel the signature of fear ⧗ of danger. This is the opposite. This is the signature of unconditional love ⧗ of absolute safety.

⧗

Take a long moment. Just sit in their presence. Feel their love for you. Feel their pride in you. Feel their profound respect for your journey, for your resilience, for the alchemist you have become. They are not here to "fix" you, because you are not broken. They are here to witness you, and to remind you of your own divine power.

⧗

Take a deep, loving breath ⧗ and in your heart, say "Thank you." Thank you for making your presence known. Thank you for your love. Know that this connection is now made. This room is now consecrated. You can return here any time, just by setting the intention. This is your quiet room. And they are always just a breath ⧗ just an invitation ⧗ away.

⧗

And now, it is time to gently return, bringing this beautiful, supportive energy back with you. With a heart full of gratitude, you can gently stand up from your chair. You give a loving nod to your sacred space ⧗ and you allow the image of the room to soften.

You are back in your golden bubble of light, but you are not alone. You are filled with a new sense* of support. Bring your awareness back to your beautiful, strong body. Feel that Fountain of Light ⧗ still breathing in the starlight ⧗ still breathing out your sanctuary.

⧗

Bring your awareness back to the physical room you are in. Feel the solid ground beneath your feet. The air on your skin. You are anchored. You are grounded. You are home in your body.

⧗

Slowly, gently, begin to bring small movements back. Wiggle your fingers, and your toes. Maybe roll your shoulders, or gently turn your head. Take a deep, cleansing breath ⧗ and let it out with a sigh.

⧗

And when you are ready, and only when you are ready ⧗ you may open your eyes.

⧗

Welcome back, alchemist. You are seen. You are loved. You are guided. You are never, ever alone.

The Daily Compass:
A 5-Minute Integration Meditation

(Music, if used, should be uplifting and gentle, but with a sense of clarity. Pacing is quicker, more direct, but still loving.)

Good morning, alchemist. Welcome to your day.

Let's begin this sacred, ordinary day with intention. Find a comfortable seat, with your spine tall and your feet flat on the floor. This is not a meditation for sleep, but for waking up for plugging in.

When you're ready, gently close your eyes.

Take one deep, cleansing breath. Inhale filling your lungs completely. And as you exhale, let go of any residue from your dreams, any static from the night. Arrive here. Now.

Let's boot up your sacred system. Imagine that brilliant, loving

"Star" of divine light shining just above your head. Take a quick, deep inhale, and draw that starlight down ⧗ down through your crown, all the way to the "Root" at the base of your spine. Feel it land, a solid, warm anchor.

⧗

Now, exhale, and push that light up your spine and out your crown, creating that strong, shimmering "Fountain of Light" that cascades all around you, instantly forming your protective, golden "Bubble of Light."

Let's do that one more time, sealing it in. Inhale, draw the "Star" light down to your "Root." Anchor. Exhale, send the light up and out, reinforcing your "Bubble." Protect.

You are now grounded and shielded in less than a minute. You are safe. You are sovereign.

⧗

Now, let's give a gentle nod to the watchman in your mind's tower. Say to him, "Thank you for your diligence. Today, you don't need to be a watchman of fear. Today, you are a seer of truth. Just be my lookout for beauty, for synchronicity, for the loving whispers."

⧗

Now, bring your awareness to your intuitive system, your "celestial radio." Imagine it in your mind. You might hear the static of the world starting up ⧗ the anxieties, the to-do lists, the emotional broadcasts of others. Acknowledge it, and then, with a conscious, intentional hand, I want you to turn the dial.

Imagine your fingers on that dial ⧖ turning it past the static ⧖ past the noise ⧖ until you hear a click ⧖ and it locks onto a single, clear, quiet frequency. It might be a hum, a feeling of peace, or a note of music. This is the frequency of your own soul. Your home frequency.

⧖

Set your intention for this frequency. Say in your heart: "Today, I am tuned to the frequency of my own spirit. I am tuned to the language of love."

⧖

Finally, let's activate your compass. Place a hand on your heart, or on your gut, wherever your "knowing" lives. Set your intention for the day:

"Today, I invite my spirit to be my compass. I will pay attention to the nudges, the whispers, the gut feelings. I will honor the feeling of a 'yes' and the feeling of a 'no.' I am not just a survivor in a chaotic world; I am an alchemist with a clear guide. I will trust the compass I was born with."

⧖

Take one last, deep, energizing breath. Feel your roots in the earth. Feel your bubble of light, strong and radiant. Feel your radio, tuned and clear. Feel your compass, active and ready.

You are not just facing the day. You are ready to create it. You are stepping out as the anchor, the channel, and the light.

Whenever you're ready, open your eyes. Go and lead with your soul.

The Alchemist's Promise

We have walked a long road together, you and I. From the darkest hallways of my past to the sacred, quiet rooms of the sanctuary we have now built within you. We have come to the end of these pages, but it is the true beginning of your alchemist's life.

The little girl who hid in the dark, the one who learned to see, feel, and know as an act of survival, could never have imagined you. She did not know that her desperate, lonely gift would one day become a map, a light to help guide you back to your own.

Your journey has its own sacred poetry. Your deepest wounds have forged your greatest strengths.

You, my dear friend, are a masterpiece of kintsugi. You are not beautiful in spite of your cracks; you are beautiful because of them. They have been filled with the gold of your own spirit, with the light of your own survival.

I see you. I honor your journey. I celebrate the magnificent, resilient, and brilliant soul that you are. Your light was never extinguished. It was just waiting for you to come home.

About the Author

Kathy Lamm is an acclaimed evidential psychic medium, artist, and author of Leave the Light On: An Alchemist's Guide to Turning Trauma into a Sacred Gift. A survivor of profound childhood neglect and abuse, she learned early on that her hyper-sensitivity was not a flaw, but a survival tool—the raw, untrained foundation of her psychic abilities. Her life's work is a testament to the alchemy that can transform our deepest wounds into our most sacred gifts.

This mission is most powerfully expressed through her internationally recognized Angel Memorial Portraits, a pro-bono service where she uses her mediumship to connect with souls who have passed—particularly children—and draws their spiritual essence for their grieving families. This act of service is the living proof of her book's core teaching: that the skills forged in trauma can be consciously honed into a powerful force for healing in the world.

With a professional background in marketing, Kathy possesses a unique ability to communicate complex spiritual and psychological concepts with clarity and compassion. She is a leading new voice in trauma-informed spirituality, committed to providing a safe, validating, and empowering path for others to reclaim their own intuitive gifts. She lives and creates in Virginia Beach, Virginia with her husband, children and grandchild.

KathyLamm.com

Kathy@KathyLamm.com